MOURNING FOR THE BRIDEGROOM
His Return. Our Hope.

Dana Candler

PUBLISHING
International House of Prayer Missions Base, Kansas City
IHOP.org

Mourning for the Bridegroom: His Return. Our Hope.
By Dana Candler

Published by Forerunner Publishing
International House of Prayer
3535 E. Red Bridge Road
Kansas City, MO 64137
forerunnerpublishing@ihop.org
IHOP.org

ISBN: 978-0-9823262-4-4

All Scripture quotations, unless otherwise marked, are from
The New King James Version, copyright © 1979, 1980, 1982
by Thomas Nelson Inc., Publishers. Used by permission.

Cover art by Seth Parks
Printed in the United States of America

Table of Contents

Dedication v

Endorsements vii

Foreword 1

CHAPTER 1: Mourning for the Bridegroom 3

CHAPTER 2: Knowing Him 19

CHAPTER 3: Embracing the Groan 33

CHAPTER 4: Beholding the One We Long For 47

CHAPTER 5: Thirsting for Him 65

CHAPTER 6: Fighting Dullness of Heart 77

CHAPTER 7: Mourning in Fasting 91

CHAPTER 8: Living as Strangers 103

CHAPTER 9: Loving His Return 117

Works Cited 129

Dedication

To my children, Madison Clairvaux, David Cairo, and Avila Hope:

With all my heart I desire that you would be true friends of the Bridegroom, those who know Jesus deeply and love Him vehemently. In a generation where sin and darkness escalate on every side, may you live worthy of the Lord, as burning and shining lamps before Him. May you gladly forsake all for the gospel, loving not your lives at any cost. And may your hearts be so anchored in the blessed hope of Christ, and your affections so riveted upon His beauty and His glory, that for love of Him you live in a continual yearning for His soon return.

Endorsements

Dana Candler is constantly exploring the great paradox of lovesickness (Song 5:8), which is a sublime mixture of exhilarated delight and distressed desire. Read contemplatively, this book will help you discover new realms of longing for Jesus.
—Bob Sorge, author, *Secrets of the Secret Place*

With clear insight, Dana boldly yet tenderly addresses the discrepancy between loving Jesus and actually longing for His return, while at the same time offering a clear road map to the lifestyle that Jesus prescribed—a lifestyle of prayer, fasting, and living hungry for Him.
—Mike Bickle, director, International House of Prayer of Kansas City

Drawing us out of the contemporary landscape where attentiveness to the glory of Christ and His coming wanes, Dana brings us alongside John, Peter, and Paul—men in whom Christ had become their all and for whom the thought of living in a perpetual state of His absence was intolerable. Dana has done much more than craft a book about intimacy with Jesus: she has recovered the forgotten heartbeat of apostolic Christianity and exposed the grand illusion that concern for His return is a matter of personal preference. May we all hear these words and truly mourn for His appearing.

—Stephen Venable, chief editor, IHOPU Press

Having read all of Dana's work, I am exceedingly thankful that she has produced, in my opinion, her finest book yet, connected to one of the most important (and oft-neglected) topics in the New Testament. I am grateful for the reach of my dear friend's heart and the manner in which she continually provokes me to examine my own life and pursuit of Jesus. What a gift to believers everywhere—Dana has gently reminded us of an aspect of life in Christ that can be a normal and glorious part of our relationship with Jesus!

—David Sliker, author, *End Times Simplified*

Jesus will return to a praying church that authentically cries, "Come, Lord Jesus!" Basing every chapter on Scripture, Dana Candler teaches us how to sustain undying love for Jesus and live with His return in mind. I have seen Dana live these truths as a teenager, college student, young married, and mother of three. Stimulating and profound, this book will make your heart beat faster for Jesus and establish an authentic urgency for the day He returns!

—David Perkins, founder, Desperation Conferences; director, World Prayer Center

This book strikingly brings together what is mistakenly separated in our thinking: intimacy with Jesus and an urgent connection to His return. This message will enflame the prayer movement worldwide. A must-read for every worship team and intercessor.

—Misty Edwards, worship leader, International House of Prayer of Kansas City

The Church finds herself today consumed with many things other than Jesus. Spending enormous amounts of time, energy, and resources on methods and "how-tos" have led to a dormant sickness in the global Body of Christ. We have forgotten the one thing needed—sitting at the feet of the One who has the words of eternal life and contains all the mysteries of both God and man. Because we know little of Him, we long little for Him. We do not mourn for Him as we should, desiring Him above all earthly pleasures and ambitions. This condition is soon to change. Before Christ's return, God's strategy will be to unfold the splendor of His Son in such a way that produces lovesickness, wholeheartedness, and exploits of faith in His people. Jesus' glory will no longer be concealed.

Even now, prophets from the wilderness are lifting their voices again: "Prepare the way of the Lord!" Dana Candler comes as one of these voices. Her work captures language for our need, and her writing comes as an antidote to our dilemma. *Mourning for the Bridegroom* will help center you on the person of Jesus and anchor you in the hope of His return. Reading this book will help fill your heart with the affections that consumed the apostles and moved them to pray, "Maranatha! Come, Lord Jesus!"

—Allen Hood, president, IHOPU

I have known Dana Candler for ten years. In this time, I have been greatly impacted by the way she lives her life before the Lord and by the way she lives her life as a wife and a mother. My heart has also been greatly impacted by the way she writes. As I began to read her new book, *Mourning for the Bridegroom*, I found that I was not only reading about Dana's journey and Dana's longing for His return; it also began to stir my own heart in a new way to watch and wait. It is as if her words walked right up to the door of my heart and took residence. I believe it will do the same for you. I highly recommend this book. "Even so, Lord, come."

—Julie Meyer, worship leader, International House of Prayer of Kansas City

Foreword

We know with certainty that before Jesus returns, a deep cry of lovesickness will grip the hearts of believers. The Church, seeing herself in her primary identity as the Bride of Christ, will globally cry, "Come!" for the return of King Jesus the Bridegroom (Rev. 22:17). While this time frame is fast approaching, we live in a day in which the Church lives largely disconnected from that intercessory cry.

Carrying a countercultural message that resists a comfortable, pragmatic brand of evangelical Christianity, *Mourning for the Bridegroom* sounds a stirring call. This book challenges Christians to bear witness to their love for Jesus, not just with their mouths, but with their holy yearning for Him. Dana urges that we understand our role as true "friends of the bridegroom" and enter into the heartfelt groan that Jesus looks for in the hour preceding His coming. With clear insight, Dana boldly yet tenderly addresses the discrepancy between loving Jesus and actually longing for His return, while at the same time offering a clear road map to the lifestyle that Jesus prescribed—a lifestyle of prayer, fasting, and living hungry for Him.

I have had the privilege of knowing and working with Dana and her husband, Matt, for many years. Both of them have been a crucial part of the leadership team at the International House of Prayer since its beginning in 1999. Over the years, I have watched as Dana continually refuses to give in to the dullness that so easily creeps up on the heart over time. She is always fighting for wholehearted abandonment in each season of life. The Lord has marked Dana with a potent message of what it means to possess authentic passion for Jesus—both the delightful aspects and the painful parts. He has given her a voice in clearly communicating and giving language to both the heart and jealous yearning for the Lord, as well as the often disillusioning twists and turns of the believer's journey in intimacy with God in this age.

I strongly recommend *Mourning for the Bridegroom* as a profound catalyst in your relationship with Jesus. Let it connect your heart to the groan that Jesus invites His friends to express during this age of faith.

Mike Bickle
Director, International House of Prayer
Kansas City, Missouri

CHAPTER ONE

Mourning for the Bridegroom

We live in the days long drawn out between the two comings of Christ. Our lives and hearts seem suspended between these different periods. It's as if one part of us reaches backward in faith, love, and remembrance to Jesus' *first* coming while the other part stretches out in expectant hope, desperate longing, and loving desire for His *second* coming. And because we truly love Him, the present delay puts us in this radical and inescapable tension of heart and soul.

Peter referred to this tension as a war of the soul (1 Pet. 2:11). Paul likened it to our living as aliens in this "present evil age" (Gal. 1:4). Jesus described it as a perpetual mourning for Himself, the Bridegroom—the inevitable suffering of soul that His friends would live in when He was no longer with them. He alluded to this when He rhetorically asked, "Can the friends of the bridegroom mourn as long as the bridegroom is with them?" (Matt. 9:15).

Jesus actually inferred by His question that we would mourn for Him. Whether we realize it or not, our present-tense lives are deeply connected to these words He spoke before His departure. He was not only thinking of the twelve disciples when He spoke of mourning for the Bridegroom. Neither was He alluding to the early church alone. He foresaw and included us. He looked through time and space and saw you and me—ones who would love Him having not seen Him, ones who would ache for Him with the sweetness of faith and hope, and ones who would wait eagerly for His return (1 Pet. 1:8). And while we live in these days of the great delay, we who love Him long for Him and fast in His absence out of deep desire for His soon coming.

Days of Delay

As Jesus looked into the eyes of His first disciples, He knew they had a unique calling—one they could not fathom. He knew the days would come when He would no longer walk the earth in bodily form and physically be among them. He understood there would be a great delay before He would come again to earth, and He was well aware of how difficult this would be for them. Because of this, Jesus prepared them for His delay by continually calling them to "watch and wait." Furthermore, He spoke parables to ready them for His going away and coming again. By no means, however, did the disciples anticipate the 2,000-year period to follow and the inevitable difficulty of heart this would bring them (Matt. 24:48, 25:5; Luke 12:35–48; 1 Thess. 4:15).

Jesus looked at His friends and knew they would never again be able to live as they used to live, for love had had its way in them, and they were ruined for anything less than the continued experience of His nearness. In the days of delay to follow, how great would be the suffering of heart for all who loved

Him, for all who knew Him as Friend! They would never again go back to life as usual. The power and the potency of their memories and their experiences with Him would cause an incessant ache to remain unanswered until they would finally see His face again and be with Him once more. Jesus understood His absence would initiate an inner groaning, a love pang for Him that would fuel their every sacrifice and empower their every service for the rest of their days. And in one sense, this is exactly how Jesus desired to leave them—and the way He desires *our* hearts to be marked—as those gripped deeply by true friendship with the kindest, the truest, the most loving, and the most *unlike-any-other* person ever to walk the earth.

Yes, Jesus knew well how this mourning would pierce every heart of all who truly love Him. And He wanted it that way. This was His plan from eternity—to so wound the hearts of His friends in love that, by sheer desire for His renewed presence and wrenching ache for Him and His return, they would far more eagerly pour out their lives in extravagant givenness to His mission. Jesus knew they would live lives worthy of the calling and usher many into the same kind of radical love for Him. In His High Priestly Prayer, Jesus mentioned those who would believe in Him because of their very testimony (John 17:20). In essence, He mentioned us.

So today, we are those who now live within the time frame stretched between the two comings of Christ. As the great drama of His plan unfolds, it's easy to feel deeply disconnected from the overall story line, to feel as though the whole drama has either concluded and we missed it or it has simply stopped. Yet this is so far from true.

When the Word took on flesh and came the first time,

revealing God and His love to the world—even unto His death on the cross—the story that began in the counsel of the Godhead before there was time thundered in climactic clarity. It did not end there, however. Advancing forward with perfect precision and unbroken stride, that great story persisted on from the cross and resurrection and the days of the early church throughout the following generations until this present day.

Often, we imagine ourselves to be estranged from this story line, as though we in our day are somehow dwelling in the aftermath of the chronicle that climaxed at the cross and resurrection—drawing upon the truths but separated from the personal participation. But that's just not true. The One who died and rose again is *alive*! He is a Bridegroom who has gone away for a time and will soon appear again—to receive His Bride to Himself (John 14:1–3). Having said yes to Him and having been joined to Him at our salvation, we are *in every way* actively involved in the drama that will soon culminate.

The same way He wounded His disciples in love by their knowing and experiencing Him is true also of us. In fact, we are invited to hold something greatly in common with all those who knew and loved Jesus at His first coming. We can share in the same fellowship of love for this same wondrous One, and as fervently as they looked and eagerly waited for His coming, our own hearts are beckoned to yearn and hope for and love His appearing (1 Cor. 1:7; 2 Tim. 4:8; 1 John 1:3).

Though Peter prophesied of the many within the Church who would scoff in these days, saying, "Where is the promise of His coming?" and who would believe that all would continue as it always had, Jesus appeals to us to view this delay in which we currently live through the lens of truth (2 Pet. 3:1–4). He wants us to see it as being redemptive and led by Him, the Lover of the ages (2 Pet. 3:8–9). The suspension between the two comings of Christ was not meant for our disillusionment but was ordained both for the salvation of many and for the full maturity of the Bride of Christ, the delay drawing forth our desperate desire for Him (2 Pet. 3:8; Rev. 22:17). He *will* come—but when He comes, will He find faith on the earth (Luke 18:8)?

Jesus looks for a very specific response from us as His friends during this time. He searches for hearts that mourn and long and fast for Him as an expression of our friendship and intimacy with Him. He seeks for those who cannot live as though things are *all right* in His absence, but rather yearn continually for His second coming. This mourning for Him and longing for His coming are produced by our growing in the knowledge of Him—the antidote that turns us from the error of a scoffing, unbelieving attitude and yields in us the assurance of all His promises (2 Pet. 3:17–18). Jesus wants the intensification of our passion and desire for Him to culminate into living blamelessly in holy love before Him. This is what He searches for even now, and this is our part to play in the great story presently unfolding.

Attentive to our every decision and our every word, Jesus desires friendship in the earth. He looks for a collective Bride that does not just pay lip service to Him, occasionally sprinkling His name into their language or *claiming* belief in Him according to convenience. He looks for those who live as though things *are actually as they are*—as though the Bridegroom that we love and will soon marry is away right now.

Though He has given us of His Holy Spirit and we know

the consolation of His indwelling presence, and though He has given us His Word and we know that which He has promised and spoken to us, the actual Person is not here in the flesh. We can't touch Him; we can't see Him with our eyes or hear Him speak with His own voice. Every day is a waiting, a preparing, and an anticipating of His most longed-for coming again. For things to go on *as they are* is not okay. John Piper states, "The Bridegroom left on a journey just before the wedding, and the Bride cannot act as if things are normal. If she loves Him, she will ache for His return" (86).

Love knows many faces. What we know of love is that it is both experientially joyful—all of the wonderful pleasures and comforts that we crave—and it is also painful; it afflicts the heart. We get wounded by love. When you love, your heart knows the paradox of experiencing both deep delight and inescapable aching. Love mourns and longs. It knows both times of delight and times of sorrow, days of joy and days of weeping. Our relationship with Jesus, the One we adore above all else, holds no exception to this reality.

Love Longs and Mourns

Anyone who has known love would not object to the notion that mourning and longing are inextricable and unavoidable parts of loving someone. In the early winter and spring of 1999, when my heart was first stirred by a boy named Matt Candler, I could have signed on every dotted line that such a notion could not be more painfully true—for better or for worse. Oh, the ache of those days! Matt and I spent much of our time away from each other, living in separate cities, and commuting only on the weekends to finally close the distance.

The weeks moved at a snail's pace, and the weekends flew feverishly by. Fridays were days of jubilation. Saturdays were a mixed jumble of emotions, both joy in being together and sorrow that our time was nearing its end. And Sundays were sorrowful even from their start as they meant the ending of our time and the beginning of yet another week apart.

In the middle of one of those long weeks, I'll never forget the time Matt called with sadness in his voice to say that, regretfully, he could not come to see me the coming weekend as we had planned due to an impending series of tests he had to study for. Suddenly my world caved in, and my mind went into a whirling and reeling, searching for another option, a compromise of sorts to somehow lessen the agony of yet another entire week of delay before seeing him again. But though I tried—offering to come there and see him between his studies or suggesting we meet halfway on Saturday, simply for lunch—Matt so sadly denied the possibility for any of my desperate proposals. And so began the long weekend apart when nothing appealed to me but moping and crying, missing and longing. No friend could comfort me, except perhaps by being a reluctant listener to hours of my talking about him.

As Friday night slowly awoke to Saturday morning, my motivations were minimal for any activities but missing Matt. I thought about getting ready for the day but could reason no purpose in it. Suddenly my room was filled with the noise of obnoxious honking and blaring music coming from below my second-story window. At only seven in the morning, I had no clue who or what this could be. Peeking out my blinds to see, I felt waves of shock and excitement hit me instantly as there stood Matt below with full smiles and laughter, looking up at me. With the news of a postponed test, he started his journey at three that morning to surprise me with the one thing that could comfort my heart—him!

This story and others like it connect us to the very point of the matter at hand. *We love a real person.* And we love Him in the way that love *loves*—missing Him when He is away and refusing comfort from anything else. He alone can answer the yearning of our hearts. He is our eternal Bridegroom who has gone away to prepare a place for us (John 14:1–2). And though He has given us His indwelling Spirit, we still long for the fullness of being face-to-face with Him, of being with Him where He is, and of beholding His glory (John 17:24).

The very role of the Holy Spirit is not simply to put us at ease in *comfort*, but to evoke deeper and stronger love for Jesus continually, even to bring about a greater and more fervent longing for Him. It's His job to prepare us for that grand day ahead when we will stand before our Bridegroom (Rev. 19:7). The Holy Spirit reminds us of what Jesus has spoken and strengthens us by telling us what is to come, taking what belongs to Jesus and declaring it to our hearts (John 14:26; 16:13–14). Just as the ancient Jewish wedding custom held that the bridegroom would always leave behind a gift for his betrothed before he left to prepare a dwelling place for her, Jesus the Bridegroom has left the gift of His own Spirit dwelling within us—so that we might be continually reminded and assured of His constant love and certain reappearing (John 14:17). The Spirit is to us a constant presence of the Lord Jesus and the One who yearns jealously to prepare us and make us worthy of Him (Jas. 4:5). He is a gift unspeakable and a gift of immeasurable worth. And yet, all of Scripture attests to the fact that this presence is but a foretaste, a down payment, and a guarantee of the fullness of *relational presence* with Jesus yet to come (2 Cor. 1:22; 6:16).

In the same way a letter from a loved one from whom we are separated brings comfort to us while at the same time afflicting our heart with a greater longing for them, so also the Spirit comforts us with the indwelling presence of Christ while simultaneously spawning a yearning for the fullness of finally seeing Him face to face (Rom 8:24; 1 Cor. 13:12). In Jesus' High Priestly Prayer, He spoke of the glory of the indwelling Spirit when He said, "I in them, and You in Me," and then just after this when He prayed, "Father, I desire that they also whom You gave Me may be with Me where I am, that they may behold My glory" (John 17:23–24). Though He is *in us* by His Spirit, Jesus cried out for His full inheritance—that all whom the Father gave Him would be with Him where He is.

We live now as those betrothed to a Bridegroom who came and paid the "dowry" for His Bride with the price of His own precious blood and has now gone away for a time (2 Cor. 11:2; Eph. 5:25–27). Awaiting us at the end of this age is a *real* wedding day, a day our natural pictures are just the depiction of. That ending marks the beginning of all beginnings and greatest joy for all the eternal ages. Yet at present, we remain in the continual tension of reaching with hearts of faith, hope, and love, not just for a new day, but for a *real face*; not just for a greater age, but for a long-awaited *embrace;* not just for a glorious kingdom, but for a *real King*.

Until that future day, our hearts do not live as though life as we know it is fine now in His absence and will get even better when He comes back. The age to come is not just a better version of *this* age. Rather, the two periods—the time of His absence and the time of His presence—stand in stark contrast and are completely opposite from one another in this one most fundamental sense: Right now, Jesus is not here. In that day, *He will be*. Right now among the nations, Jesus is not adored. He is not declared worthy. He is not given the incessant worship that is due Him. But one day, *He will be* (Zech. 14:16; Phil. 2:10). Right now, our children do not live in a culture that magnifies the splendor of His person and worships Him as the Most High God, but one day, *they will*. Right now, sickness and pain, mistreatment and the grinding of the poor and the weak pervade the nations. Yet when He comes and rules in righteousness, such atrocities will be no more (Rev. 21:3–4).

Until that day, any degree of comfort, joy, and delight we know is fixed and adjoined to the immovable anchor of hope in the person of Jesus and the day of His appearing (Titus 2:13; Heb. 6:19). We have known foretastes but yearn for the fullness to come. Right now, we live by faith. Then, we shall live by sight (2 Cor. 5:7). Right now, we hope for what we cannot see. Then, hope shall be no more, for hope that is seen is not hope (Rom. 8:24). Right now, we love One that our eyes have never seen (1 Pet. 1:8). Then, we shall see face-to-face and know as we are known (1 Cor. 13:12).

The Dilemma before Us

Yes, love always pines and yearns when the beloved is absent, and we—as those who love Jesus in the time between His advents—are in every way subject to such longing. Yet this brings us to a dilemma—a difficulty with a certain sting to it. The dilemma is that though our minds know He was here and then taken up to heaven—and our mouths may give testimony to being His Bride awaiting His return—the longing of our hearts for Him is disproportionate to the time we are in. The difficulty is that though we claim deep love for Jesus, the degree of our satisfaction in the way things are indicates we might be guilty of a grave error in the laws of love. Yes, we do love Jesus. But if we love Him so, shall we not also miss Him greatly in His absence? Shall we not long for His appearing because He is the One we cannot live without? The sting that we must receive comes when we put this question to ourselves: could it be that our lack of mourning for Him might be significantly tied to our lack of truly knowing Him?

The fact is we long for proximity and despise estrangement from those we love. If we truly love another, an aching and mourning must accompany any separation from that beloved one. Otherwise, there might exist good grounds for questioning if it was truly love at all or if we actually know the one we "love." And *if* somehow this satisfied-in-separation condition was in fact some version of love, it is one that we would not readily nor willingly recognize. For what husband loves his wife and yet lives undisturbed and untroubled if she is taken from him? Will he not fight day and night to bring her back, all the while sick in his heart in each day of separation? What wife is indifferent to her husband's being drafted off to war? Will she not live each day in an unrelenting ache for his return?

If we are willing in humility to bring our own hearts into question, we might find that *we* are the ones violating love's laws. The very thing that Jesus searches for, the very thing that He refuses to come back without, is a rare find in all the earth. It is the heart of a yearning Bride in deep affection for an absent

Bridegroom and in continual longing for His appearing, not just occasional pining.

In his book, *Systematic Theology*, Wayne Grudem articulates this dilemma well:

> Do Christians in fact eagerly long for Christ's return? The more Christians are caught up in enjoying the good things of this life, and the more they neglect genuine Christian fellowship and their personal relationship with Christ, the less they will long for his return . . . To some extent, then, the degree to which we actually long for Christ's return is a measure of the spiritual condition of our own lives at the moment (1093).

Somehow we, as the Body of Christ in our day, have used our theology to separate ourselves from the real person of Christ. We call His second coming *eschatology*, attempting to determine the manner and timing of it. We choose our stance on the end times accordingly. We receive the Jesus of the first coming, but we retreat and hesitate when it comes to His second coming, willing to call it irrelevant to the present time. Yet in all of this we forget what cannot be forgotten. We forget that He is a real person. He is alive and even now sits at the right hand of the Father, waiting for the day when His enemies will be made His footstool (Heb. 10:13). In Jesus' first coming, He took on flesh, and even now possesses a resurrected body, not merely a spirit. He will come again to the earth in bodily form—the living God incarnate (Acts 1:9–11; Phil. 3:21). In some ways, this reminder of Jesus' eternal incarnation helps our hearts connect to just how alive He is in this very moment.

And we forget, above all, that the second coming is far more than a set of ideas. It is deeply personal. Love does not choose timeframes, but persons. We do not love an age, but a Man who is God. And we do not love part of His existence, but the whole of it. If I were to love my children for only part of their lives and then from that point only ever speak of their childhood, their teenage years, and their young-adult days, never continuing on with them in the years to follow, would I truly be loving them? To love a person is to love them not in segments, but in entirety. Because we love Him, we embrace with affection what we have already known and seen while, at the same time, not stopping short of pouring out our eager expectation and longing of what is yet to come.

Though we claim to love Jesus deeply and though we rightly say that He is our *everything*, when it comes to His return, the truth of the matter, if exposed, is that we may not really want Him to come back, at least not yet. Though we speak of His glorious appearing, part of us does not really want it to occur in our day. Why? Because in our heart of hearts, we do not want a disruption of the lives we are living nor the trouble that we know surrounds His coming. We cling to comfort and do not like trouble or the unknown. We much prefer the idea of long and full lives, of raising our children and our grandchildren in peace and safety, of living comfortably until we finally die of old age and go to heaven. Our lives bear witness that we favor *this* future more than the dramatic transition of two ages, the troubles prophesied, the testing spoken of, and the suffering foretold in the time frame of Jesus' reappearance (Matt. 24; Luke 21:7–36). Yet once again, love does not know this sort of option. Love longs in absence and does not settle into separation.

A Time to Mourn

Here we are in the days torn in the tensions that Jesus knew so well would arrive. The signs of the times pound upon our doors, and the churning of the nations along with the surging of evil seduction rages all around us. We are not to sweep these signs under the rug and find solace in the reasoning that we cannot know the time of Jesus' return (Matt. 24:36; 25:13; Mark 13:32–37). Such a response neglects the very heartbeat of Jesus' plea to be watchful for every sign and any movement or indication of His coming. In this trembling time frame, the fiery eyes of the enthroned Bridegroom search for the light of burning mournfulness and continual watchfulness within the hearts of His friends—within the lives of His Bride. He will not come within a vacuum. He will not come once more without that groan. Though He will come as a thief to those who are of the night, to the sons of light and of the day He will come as an answer to their own aching expectation (1 Thess. 5:4–10).

For all those who truly love Jesus, it is a time to mourn. Why? As simply as He Himself put it, because *He is not here* (Matt. 9:15). It is because He has been taken from us. We are not to live as though things are all right in His absence, as though we are any more content than we would be if betrothed to one from whom we were separated. Rather than growing accustomed to the separation, He urges us to constantly remain in yearning and expectation for Him. If in fact we love Him as we say we do, living in a burning ache and continual groan for Him and for His appearing is the only fitting posture of heart.

Jesus has given us His Holy Spirit to both console our hearts in the midst of the delay and to produce in us the very mourning that He seeks. The Spirit will awaken a growing yearning within us for Jesus. He will bring a strong hunger to full maturity in the hearts of the Bride of Christ worldwide, this mourning ultimately hastening the Day of the Lord (2 Pet. 3:12). Jesus will return in direct *response* to this swelling, consuming cry of, "Come, Lord Jesus!" And this age will move toward its consummate end as our great mourning and yearning finally meet their consolation in the second advent of Jesus (Rev. 22:17).

Here is where we find our invitation. Jesus' searching eyes look for a resting place in us, and His jealous heart refuses to leave us in anything less than radical love for Him. Part of that love finds its expression in longing and mourning and fasting in His absence. Because we love Him, it is time to mourn for Him. Yet this longing does not arise out of nowhere. It is a direct outflow of having seen and truly known Him. Thus, it is only as the Spirit opens our eyes to see Him and know Him *as He is*—in all of His matchless beauty and unsearchable riches—that fervent love will grip our hearts and transform our inklings of desire into true passion and compelling longing for Him (Eph. 1:16; 3:8; Rom. 5:5; 9:5).

CHAPTER TWO

Knowing Him

You can only miss someone you know. You can only long for someone you truly love. As simple as that sounds, we must be reminded that longing for Jesus is merely the outcome of having known and loved Him. Longing and mourning are the fruit of real relationship. You cannot work up an aching for Jesus in your own soul, somehow convincing yourself that you are supposed to be unsatisfied right now and thus forcing your emotions into a state of discontentment.

Like my personal story, I didn't miss Matt because I was *obligated* to. Rather, I just began to know and love him and, consequently, missed him during the times when we were apart. This "missing him" became the inevitable result of that knowledge and love.

It's the same way with Jesus. We do not hunger for Jesus out of a void, but out of relationship. We do not ache out of emptiness or absence, but out of knowledge and experience. We crave more of that which we have known and tasted and experienced in His love. Out of that place of familiarity and fellowship, we say, "I have to have more. I cannot be content with the memory of what I've known, but I must know more and more, even unto fullness." This is what happened to the apostles of the Lamb who knew Him well, heard His words, saw His eyes of compassion, and felt His heart of kindness. And this is where each of us is called to live continually. For having not yet seen Him with our eyes, we *do* love Him, believing He is most precious (1 Pet. 1:7–8).

Longing out of Presence

There is a certain longing a man might have for his future spouse before he ever meets her or shares in his first conversation with her. Yet this cannot be compared even slightly to the deep ache he finds after being married to her for many years and being apart from her due to some circumstance of separation. Our longing for Jesus is analogous to this picture. The ache we experience prior to deeply knowing Jesus, the innate craving within every human person, compares to the certain "missing" we might experience when we long for companionship and have not yet met or known our future love. This is a real desire that cannot be ignored. Yet it cannot really compare to the desire that comes not out of absence, but out of presence—not out of a relational void, but out of a relational wealth. Once that missing takes on a real face and name—once one's heart is connected to a *person* with real qualities, particularities, and idiosyncrasies, and, in fact, that missing is returned, then yearning is reciprocated—then begins the craving out of presence, the desire flowing from communion.

Shedding insight on the difference between this longing that flows out of presence and the longing that exudes from emptiness, Henri Nouwen writes:

> In the spiritual life we have to make a distinction between two kinds of loneliness. In the first loneliness, we are out of touch with God and experience ourselves as anxiously looking for someone or something that can give us a sense of belonging, intimacy, and home. The second loneliness comes from an intimacy with God that is deeper and greater than our feelings and thoughts can capture.
>
> We might think of these two kinds of loneliness as two forms of blindness. The first blindness comes from the absence of light, the second from too much light. The first loneliness we must try to outgrow with faith and hope. The second we must be willing to embrace in love (30).

When we long for God, it is because we have known Him, if even in the smallest measure, enough to have our souls stirred with a craving for more of Him. We cannot crave something fully unless we have first tasted of it. Even thirst for Jesus—though it begins with that very first thirst that He placed innately in our being, that craving for the Infinite that we were born with—takes on a whole new life when it flows out of encounter with Him. Once we have tasted of Jesus in even the smallest way, tasting and seeing that He is good, this taste becomes for us that which fuels our hunger and our pursuit of greater encounter (Ps. 34:8; 1 Pet. 2:3).

God cultivates hunger in us by first awakening us with His precious nearness. We begin to know a real person, the person of Jesus, and that knowing spawns a deep craving for an even greater experience and greater depth of relating to and with Him. Over time, as love grows within us, so too does our desire for Him. It is this desire that burns in us as a living flame, one born in the fires of true relationship, eventually extinguishing every lesser longing and taking over the whole of our affections.

Knowing Him Means Longing for Him

To enter into the place of longing and mourning for God, we find but one avenue. We must come to know the person of Christ. And this is where Jesus stands so unequaled and so unique. We were made for Him and fashioned to be answered only in Him. When the human heart seeks Him willingly, and, in so doing, discovers even the smallest fragments of insight into His heart, the most automatic heart-response is an unyielding desire to have Him in fullness. Every taste of Him leads the heart into a greater cry for *more*. To any degree that we have experienced or seen Him, a yearning for a greater touch and vision of Him is awakened within us. One taste of Jesus and His love and one is ruined. How great the *potency* of Jesus' love upon the human heart, of the ability of its power to wound and ruin a soul in love with one single taste (1 Pet. 2:3)! This one word, *taste*, gives evidence of the power and force of this holy love. One drink and one cannot forget, cannot return to the comforts of yesterday, and cannot forsake the pursuit of a greater tasting.

In my own experience, I find myself struck by the reality that perhaps I've only ever had but a single taste of Him. My knowing of Him, when measured by the delight of the eternal ages, is so small, and I've experienced Him so little, barely witnessing His delights, His beauty, and His satisfactions. In the ages to come, I know that I will look back at this point in my journey and see clearly just how modest my experience of His love was, just how slight my seeing of His beauty was. And yet, here lies the potency of the love I have had but a foretaste of: *one taste* has ruined me, has wounded me, for life. One taste has sent me out into the wilderness, has pushed me out into the unknown, and continually frees me to forsake the cares of this life by the sheer pressure of the pull on my heart for more of Him.

The world and all of its trinket-pleasures and stifling satisfactions require great excess and overloading to touch the human person; at the same time, having extracted all possible pleasure, one is left still painfully unsatisfied and greatly disillusioned from these empty and broken cisterns (Jer. 2:13). But Jesus—the opposite is true of Him! One taste and we are wounded with love; one touch and we are ruined for anything less. So potent is His love, so piercing is His touch that one slight encounter of Him is enough sweetness to send us searching for Him all of our days, refusing the comforts of this world and reaching with arms outstretched toward the eternal pleasures and fulfillments found solely in Him.

One touch of His love and our hearts refuse to live happily ever after except in His presence. We mourn in our hearts with an ache unanswered apart from His nearness. This ache remains with us constantly in an age where we live as the betrothed Bride awaiting the Bridegroom's return for us. We come to the place where, refusing every earthly comforter that comes knocking on our door to soothe our swelling yearning, we wait for *Him* alone (Ps. 77:2).

Longing with the Bridegroom

When Jesus came in the flesh and dwelt among us, He displayed openly the God of all human history who had continually revealed Himself to His people Israel as a Husband pursuing His wayward Bride (Isa. 54:5; Jer. 3:14; Hos. 2:16). The God of the Old Testament who had repeatedly made Himself known as a jealous Husband, yearning for His peoples' affections and marriage covenant, now stepped onto the scene of human history in the flesh, declaring openly that He is the Bridegroom and we are His Bride (Matt. 9:15; 22:2–14; 25:1–13)! When Jesus took on flesh and lived among us, ultimately laying down His life for us upon the cross, the One who had been veiled and obscure in times past suddenly radiated before our eyes in unabashed affection and consuming love. He opened the door of His covenantal promises made to Abraham to both Jew and Gentile through the rending of His flesh (Eph. 2:15). He is a Bridegroom, and He came to pay the price for His Bride—the high cost of His own precious life.

The Son of Man who walked the dusty roads of Israel over 2,000 years ago has not changed in His heart, has not ceased to exist, has not Himself somehow just resumed life as it was in the eternal ages before His first coming. Rather, He sits as God enfleshed and enthroned even now at His Father's right hand, with scars upon His hands giving witness, and groans of intercession giving voice to the ever-burning flame raging in His heart. He is a Bridegroom who laid down His life for His beloved. For the joy set before Him, He endured the cross and, even now, from His place at the right hand of the Father, He intercedes incessantly until His enemies are made His footstool (Heb. 12:2). The One who introduced Himself as the Husband of His people at His first coming is still a Bridegroom awaiting the day of the gladness of His heart (Song 3: 11).

You cannot believe Jesus is truly a Bridegroom without also believing His heart moves as one. The two go hand-in-hand. If we have come so far as to see Him in this light and to believe this about who He is, then we must also ask, "And what of His heart right now? Can a bridegroom forget his bride? Can a bridegroom go away and forget his wedding day? Can a bridegroom leave his betrothed bride without also leaving his heart?" Thus, we know by His own establishing Himself before us in the identity of a bridegroom that Jesus' heart could not be more involved, more active, or more attuned to this unfolding drama and to the dear ones that He so loves who live right now in the walls of time, the groans of delay, and the oppositions of this present evil age. Just as He urges us, He Himself remains continually in the place of longing and waiting until the glorious day when His return will split the skies and His reign will make all things right. He has not disconnected from the story and by no means is He detached from the drama at hand.

In the midst of what to us is such a prolonged delay, we lose touch with the great story of which we are a part. Yet to the One who calls one day like a thousand years and a thousand years like one day, we have only just begun (2 Pet. 3:8). What drove Him to the cross still looms before His vision, still hovers continually before His gaze. He's looking for voluntary love from our hearts, and He's waiting for the day when He will come again and receive us to Himself that we might be with

Him where He is (John 14:2–3).

When He calls us to love Him with our yearning, He calls us to live where *He* lives. Though our brokenness and pride often flee from the place of longing and aching at the heart level, love leaves us no options. When Jesus prayed in John 17:24, "Father, I desire that they also whom You gave Me may be with Me where I am," He voiced the eternal longing and yearning in the heart of God. And with this prayer, He conveyed His fervent desire that He even now burns with, for it yet remains to be answered in fullness.

The Lord calls us not just to feel the pangs of this ache occasionally, but to live with them continually. The way that He sustains us during our ache is by revealing to us that He Himself is yet aching for us and He wants us to join Him in the place of longing and desire. He is the Bridegroom. We are the Bride. And we are yearning in the time between the two advents, the time between the two comings. His desire was not complete at the resurrection but reaches forward to the fullness. Continually He cries, "Father, I desire. Father, I desire. Father, I desire . . ." (John 17:26).

Hopeful Mourning

Gloomy people with sad faces—this might be the first impression that comes to our minds when we think of mourning and what it might look like. What strikes us initially would be in the realm of the emotions—in the tears and in the sorrows. Yet mourning for Jesus touches far more than our emotions, and even *in* the realm of emotions, it cannot be limited to tears and sorrows. Jesus' invitation to mourn for Him as the Bridegroom does not fit under the gloomy definitions and images we might initially think of. He does not invite us to possess a pessimistic, joyless, semi-depressed outlook on life, nor to be bound by a sadness that leads to apathy rather than action. He does not call us to hopelessness or to a melancholic view of things as they are. All of this cannot be what we think of when we hear the call to mourn for the Bridegroom.

Longing and mourning for Jesus reveals connection to true reality. It means that while the world is caught up in the seduction of momentary pleasures, their center of gravity being this temporal age and all its fleeting passions, cares, and dreams, we are caught up and riveted upon the person of Christ, with all of our passions and dreams being set upon *Him* (1 Pet. 1:13). This being the case, we are torn in the tensions of an undeniable delay as this One we adore and worship is not esteemed and acclaimed among the nations. He alone is worthy of all worship, and yet He remains the One most rejected and hated among the peoples. He must be set in His rightful place before all men as the Lord of lords. He must be revered rightly—as the "Desire of All Nations" (Hag. 2:7). One day, He will be. This establishing of the One we love to His rightful place and reverence among the nations is the great day that we long and yearn for and set our hope upon. This hope we have is not just a vain pining or an illusory wish. It is certain and upheld by the strength and faithfulness of God. Thus, our hope does not carry with it the possibility of despair but is filled with rejoicing (Rom. 12:12; 2 Thess. 2:16). It *will* one day be fully realized (Rom. 8:25; Heb. 6:11, 18; 10:23).

We could say that, if mourning for the Bridegroom is to be biblical, with its motivations rooted in sound theology, it is the furthest thing from hopelessness. In fact, it is anchored entirely in the certainty of our future hope (Heb. 6:19). It is the furthest thing from depressive sorrows. It is the outworking in the present age of having touched and known the foretastes of the age to come and the *King* to come. It is the furthest thing from joyless living. It means our joys are simply in another place. Rather than being caught up and pacified by the delights of this age, we are completely unmoved by them; we are ruined and wrecked by the far superior joys of the person of Jesus, unwilling to be satisfied except in Him alone (Phil 3:7–10).

Can you imagine Paul ever being rightly accused of hopelessness or joylessness? His life resounded with the theme of rejoicing in hope, rejoicing in all things, and living with eager expectation of what is to come (Rom. 5:2; 12:12; 1 Cor. 1:7; Phil. 4:4). Imagine what kind of supernatural joy Peter knew personally as He spoke of rejoicing even while we are in the midst of various trials—even though we do not see Jesus—with a joy inexpressible and full of glory (1 Pet. 1:6, 8). These men were true friends of the Bridegroom. And oh, how they mourned and yearned for Him. Yet this mourning did not burden them with depressing gloom or immobilize them into passivity, but motivated them for mission and urged them to give all for the gospel. This incessant flame burned in them continually as they awaited their all-consuming passion—Christ Himself in fullness—and looked for Him to be worshiped and adored, as He deserved.

It must be clear that this mourning for Jesus is not only sadness. Let's consider what we know intuitively in our relationships with one another. When we love someone and he is away, part of our mourning his absence means enjoying and celebrating him even when not with him. We remember his glory, think on what we love about him, laugh aloud at memories or words treasured in our hearts. Mourning includes both tears of painful joy and separation; we feel bereft of the one dearly loved. We miss because we *joy* in someone, and part of our missing is simply delighting in who he is, doing things that remind us of him, living our "little moments" as though in his presence and for his enjoyment.

All of this translates so effortlessly to our relationship with Jesus and is taken to the highest level in that application. Because we love Him, we *do not* forget Him, and that continual remembrance manifests in both delighting in Him and yearning for Him. We, indeed, love a real person—the most glorious person alive. He is God Himself, who took on flesh and came once to walk and live among us. For all those who witnessed Him, He was touchable, visible, tangible, real. And to all who knew Him as friend and Lord, He was to their souls matchless in the splendors of His person. His presence produced an indescribable joy coupled with an insatiable hunger for more.

Desiring Him is unlike desiring any other, for no other is actually able to answer the full craving of the human person. He Himself is the end of all our wanting. Longing for Him is the acknowledgement that He alone is true joy, true comfort, and true satisfaction. He Himself is our blessed hope (Titus 2:13). We joy and delight in Him above all else, and because of this, we have true and undeniable foretastes of delight, joy, and pleasure. Yet even these have within them the continual aftertaste of heartache in that we long for *more* of Him. Our tasting of Him is true joy and simultaneously deeper yearning for the foretaste to be met with fullness.

Embracing the Ache

The saints throughout history called this divine tasting "a wound of love." For our tasting of Him leaves behind a painful, burning, incessant, and incurable wound that will not leave the heart alone and will not allow it to return to the old chasings. These divine wounds of love perfectly impair us from living satisfied in a world of fabricated pleasures, leaving us profoundly unfulfilled until we finally see the face for which we long and know the true beauty for which we have forsaken all. We are left as pilgrims, just as the Lord planned, wandering as strangers in this life, just as He so desired.

This is why John of the Cross cried out, "Why, since you wounded this heart, don't you heal it? And why, since you stole it from me, do you leave it so, and fail to carry off what you have stolen?" (45). Why does the Lord wound us only? Why wouldn't He go much further with His wooing and somehow carry off the whole of us, rather than ruining us so deeply and then leaving us to wander in this wilderness, waiting for His return? This wound of love, brought about by the potency of but one taste of knowing Jesus, is the brilliant tool found in the hand of God to win over the fickle human heart. This tool chips away at the hardness and transforms it from its disloyal dividedness into the flaming faithfulness descriptive of those He calls "friends of the Bridegroom."

One taste is all we need to ruin us for anything less, to make us loyally His alone. If we embrace so holy a wound, we will be led over time to yet another taste of Him, and another, and yet another. These tastes only wound us more in love for Him until, missing Him so much, we are immune from the pounding of other lovers upon our doors. O painful and precious wound that leaves us all alone except for when we find the One in whom our soul loves! O precious wound that compels us to love Him wholly and not in part! It is this wound that urges us to count all else as loss for the sake of knowing Him—until we are finally healed of so great an ache with the beauty of His holy face.

Living in this constant ache of love and longing—all flowing from having known and experienced Jesus in the beauty and matchlessness of who He is—is the mourning that He is after in our hearts. Even now, as Jesus sits upon the throne, He searches the earth with His holy and precious eyes—the Man with the eyes of fire. He searches for those who would volunteer their love freely (Ps. 110:3). He searches for worshipers (John 4:23). He searches for those wholly given unto Him. Part of that givenness and part of that love are characterized by our knowing and living in the painful longing of His present absence.

To genuinely taste of Jesus is to be wounded in love for Him, and to genuinely know Him is to long for Him. We have tasted of Him, and in that tasting, we long for fullness. We live hungry for the only Person that our lives depend upon and for the only One who can answer the longing in our souls. And even in this time and place of hunger, we must recognize the Lord's hand. He Himself has given this ache to us as a gift and beckons us to receive it with all our hearts. Though this means embracing even the less comfortable and less pleasurable facets of love, and though we may encounter a certain sting in our hearts, we know that even these less enjoyable aspects are still undeniably true and essential expressions of authentic love and friendship with Jesus.

CHAPTER THREE

Embracing the Groan

As was noted previously, longing and aching for God never come from our own conjuring. We did not invoke this ache. He did. It originated in His heart. If we want to stay in the place of hunger, we must understand this, or else we will lose our way. Yearning for God does come with a certain holy sting that we must know how to navigate. It is for this reason that we must recognize our ache for what it is—a gift of God given in direct answer to our prayers for more of Him.

That the Lord would purposefully produce something as painful as hunger and mourning—that He would actually *want* to do this—may be a difficult concept for us to embrace. Are we ready to come to terms with and even welcome this idea—that the Lord would deliberately instigate a separation from Himself so as to produce in us the rawness and richness of love that only *parting* can cause? When we love someone, we will drive any distance, cross any barrier, and bridge any chasm in order to get to the one we love. This is the element of love that the God who is leading history has brought so forcefully to the surface by setting Himself on display before our eyes, causing us to see and love Him, manifesting His love so unutterably on the cross, and then departing from us for a time.

A Sign of Presence

It's important to note that Jesus has not left us here to mourn and groan while He has gone away in blissful indifference. If we are not careful, we will interpret the pain that we experience—the very pain meant to deepen our love for Him—as the Lord's rejection of us, rather than the direct workings of His love within us. We can always be assured that any degree of longing for Jesus that we experience originated with the Lord Himself (1 John 4:19). We only love because He *first* loved, and we only long for Jesus because He *first* longed for us and set His affections upon us. Our desire is but an echo of His own desire, and any degree to which we find ourselves actually hungering for Him finds its source in His own desire and longing. Because of this truth, we can rest assured that we do not mourn for the Bridegroom in isolation but in the fellowship of intimacy with Him. We can be confident in the covenant love of Jesus for us, embracing the ache as part of our relationship, rather than scorning it as a sign of His rejection.

Our hearts are prone towards offense, distance, and distrust. And perhaps nothing causes an influx of cynicism like the pain of a heart openly waiting for God, feeling denied or rejected. In our aching for God, we so often interpret the raw wound of hunger as the Lord's absence from us. We possess a deep wanting for more of Him, and yet, even in the experience of that want, we find a slight offense toward Him waiting impatiently in the wings for whenever we can endure such pain no longer. Here is where our quick surrender to offense has deceived us. When we do not find Him after hungering for Him, we turn to the accuser who charges God with indifference, and we side with him. All the while, the One whom we so readily accuse was not absent at all but *tangibly present*. He was with us in the hunger. He was drawing us to Himself through the yearning.

Perhaps it is rare to think of longing as a sign of fellowship and proof of presence rather than an indication of solitude and absence. But such is the case with our longing for Jesus. We were fashioned as ones who relentlessly thirst and hunger for a God who is infinite. As such, any longing we experience for Him expresses this God-given ache and is in itself a gift and a favor offered to the heart by the Lord. He gives us the very love with which to love Him (John 17:26). No man comes to Jesus unless the Father draws him (John 6:44). We only ever love Him and long for Him because He first loved and longed for us (1 John 4:19). Consequently, we do not *decide* to be in love, but we are escorted by love itself to places we would have never planned or thought conceivable, sacrificing in ways we would have never dreamed possible.

Receiving the Gift

Truly, one of God's greatest gifts to the human heart is that of hunger—to any who will take its precious aching into her possession. A gift beyond greatest measure is given to those who truly desire to know Jesus, to love this One whom our eyes have never seen (1 Pet. 1:8). It is the gift of a groan, a given and received ache that is granted by the hand of divine love Himself. When the skies break open at His return and He begins to establish His kingdom on the earth, this groan shall be granted its answer; the gift of mourning will be met in fullness with the promised blessing of eternal comfort amid the glorious and peaceful reign of Jesus' everlasting kingdom (2 Sam. 7:12; Dan. 7:27; Matt. 5:4; 2 Tim. 4:8). Until that day, it remains for the soul of the believer as an ever-present reminder—an unrelenting remembrance of the One whom we love, the One for whom we are made, and the One to whom we are going.

Of this gift, so needed, Jesus said:

> Blessed are you who hunger now, for you shall be filled. Blessed are you who weep now, for you shall laugh . . . But woe to you who are rich, for you have received your consolation. Woe to you who are full, for you shall hunger. Woe to you who laugh now, for you shall mourn and weep. (Luke 6:21–25)

Knowing the propensity for us to allow our hearts to become stifled and taken captive by a thousand lesser loves, Jesus proclaimed a blessing over those willing to stay the course in the rigors of hungering after God. He knew that without this aching, our hearts would become content with the temporal things that give momentary pleasure. Though the cry of our lips may be, "Oh, God, all I want is You," the state of our soul—being so stuffed with the things of this world, the cares of this life, and even all the pleasures that are good, yet inferior—leaves us incapable of actually being deeply satisfied, deeply quenched, and deeply answered in Jesus.

Those who hunger now are blessed because, without this ache, we subtly settle into business-as-usual in this present age and become dangerously lulled to sleep. Though created to touch transcendence, we are shockingly content with trivialities. Though made for perfect and holy love, we are startlingly appeased by replicas of true relationship. Thus, how great our need for a holy rumbling from deep within that refuses to be silenced until answered in Jesus. Nothing keeps the heart awake like dissatisfaction, just as nothing keeps the body from sleep like the gnawing of hunger's growl within. The one who is full is the one who does not think to look for something higher or greater—no matter how appealing.

Truly the gift is in the groan. Here in the center and thick of the Western world, steeped in a culture that is so counter to the ways of God, dulled by a thousand unnecessary stimulants, you and I have capacities that from God's perspective might resemble shriveled up raisins. We are so dried up by our pursuit of lesser things, so clouded by that which is temporal, that we have no capacity for the eternal and no room for God. And this is where the gift of hunger plays its part so well.

I remember when the Lord initially began to disrupt my life by revealing to me the principle that He gives more according to my hunger for more, and that until my capacity was enlarged by spiritual hunger, I would be limited in my experience of God. I thought I was waiting on Him to come and reveal Himself in greater measure to me, yet all the while it was He who waited on me. He was waiting for the hunger that He demands. He refuses to give anything except on the basis of hunger, and that hunger is not hunger unless it is for a time *unanswered.*

Though I have known Jesus my whole life, I had never considered that I lacked this inward groan. My heart's capacity was paltry, but I did not know it. I thought I loved God intensely, but He revealed to me that, in all truth, my thirst for Him was relatively inconsequential. And this exposure was truly a gift. At that time, I entered into what I now call "the longing to long" or "the hunger to hunger." I was in that tension between sincerely wanting to want God and not yet being overcome by hunger for Him—and this is exactly where God wanted me. Hunger begets hunger, and, in time, He would cause my initial desire to give way to strong desire—that He might answer me with more of Himself, just as He loves to do.

On this subject of longing and hungering for the Lord, A. W. Tozer wrote:

> I want deliberately to encourage this mighty longing after God. The lack of it has brought us to our present low estate. The stiff and wooden quality about our religious lives is a result of our lack of holy desire. Complacency is a deadly foe of all spiritual growth. Acute desire must be present or there will be no manifestation of Christ to His people. He waits to be wanted. Too bad that with many of us He waits so long, so very long, in vain . . . O God, I have tasted Thy goodness, and it has both satisfied me and made me thirsty for more. I am painfully conscious of my need of further grace. I am ashamed of my lack of desire (18, 20).

It is the hungry that God satisfies, and those who long and mourn that He fills and comforts. Thus, the blessing of hungering after God is in the way it prepares us for more of Him and carves out our capacity, once so stifled, to receive Him. When Jesus declared, "Blessed are you who hunger now," He pronounced blessing upon the ones who receive this gift of aching immediately, in the here and now. He said in essence, "Blessed are you because your joy is coming. You have taken all of your affections and centralized them upon the person who is joy and consolation *Himself.* And when the others are weeping, you will be laughing and rejoicing. I am the only One who remains, and I am joy—joy unspeakable. I am the answer, the consolation, the filling. I AM. And blessed are you if you hunger for Me. Blessed are you if you weep for Me. Blessed are you if you mourn for Me, because you will be filled. You will be answered."

Truly, the Lord purposed this groan not for our difficulty but as a way of keeping our hearts awake when they are most prone towards sleeping. This mourning and aching is far more powerful than just an emotion and far stronger than just a sentiment. It is a way of life and a state of being. It is a longing that orders every facet of our existence, fueling faithfulness and obedience and humility. The inner groan keeps our hearts in love for God and reaching for eternity so that we might flee the deception of the lusts of this age and the comforts of the temporary. In this way, this groan is one of our greatest assets in this life, in this moment called time. It is for us as a helper, to refine our resolutions and make good our intentions in God.

A Costly Call

The nature of the human heart is to despise pain. We run from adversity, flee from sorrow, and do whatever we can to avert difficulty. It is the most natural response of the human heart to avoid pain and suffering and to reach for comfort, joy, and pleasure instead. We do this in *all* realms of life—from the physical, where we do not like the feeling of hunger or weakness; to the relational, where we seek to avoid conflict and defend our hearts against rejection or heartache; to the practical, where we construct our lives in an effort to steer clear of conflicts in every dimension. In our prayer lives and intimacy with God, this natural aversion shows up quite frequently. We despise waiting on the Lord without immediate answer and are so quickly apt to settle for a mediocre pursuit rather than a radical one, because we are afraid of the pain, so fearful of the cost, and reluctant to embrace the rigors of truly being abandoned unto God.

This reach for joy and pleasure in itself is not wrong, but natural, even surfacing in our wanting to escape hell and go to heaven. However, the question must be posed: is our desire to enter such joy and peace motivated by better circumstances or by the person of Jesus—the One who is the only good, the only joy, and the only source of true and everlasting pleasure? We all desire to avoid pain, yes, but this is not why we say yes to Christ. He is not the means to better circumstances, but the end in Himself. And though He does not call us to enjoy pain or sorrows, He greatly longs for us to choose Him at all costs.

This is where the nature of man and the nature of love come into conflict and go their separate ways like an inflexible fork in the road. Man in his depravity goes one way—his own self-preserving way—and love in its glory goes another—the way of self-sacrifice and self-denial. Man seeks, at all costs, to do whatever he can to shield himself from pain. Love seeks, at all times, to avail itself wholly, to embrace every wound and every ache without observance of price, willing to go to any lengths in longsuffering and selflessness for another. And it is here that the Lord brings us to the place of choice: whether or not to choose and embrace Him even though it so chafes our natural inclinations.

When Jesus entered our existence as a Man, having taken in fullness our humanity, He did that which no man had ever done before and no man could ever do again except through Him: He loved in the fullness of self-sacrifice while living in the frail confines of humanity. The forceful tide of humanity's bent toward self-protection and self-preservation, even at the expense of others, had no pull upon Him. Jesus was wounded in every way—in heart, in relationship, in circumstance, in reputation, and in body. But, in every way, He neither evaded it nor fled from it. He faced such woundedness head-on with forehead set, not shrinking back from any invitation toward greater love and greater sacrifice (Is. 50:7). Why? Certainly not because there is any intrinsic good in pain or suffering. No, it was all for the sake of the vision that continually hung before His distant gaze—the joy that was set before Him (Heb. 12:2).

And this vision He also sets before our eyes. This heart He asks us to embrace, thus calling us to live where He lives (Phil. 2:5; Heb. 12:3). He stands at that inflexible fork in the road and bids us to love Him as He has loved us, to befriend Him as He first befriended us, and to follow Him down the road that only love travels. It is a costly road and means refusing the comfort of self-preservation and allowing for the vulnerability of love. Yet, as Paul reminds us, the excellence of knowing Him so far surpasses any price we might pay or loss we might incur (Phil. 3:7–8). Our gaze is set upon the joy of knowing Him and the everlasting union with Him, forever minimizing the momentary troubles that we undergo in such pursuit (2 Cor. 4:17).

Though There Be a Sting

As I have given myself and my heart to the vulnerability of this heart posture through the years, many pitfalls and difficulties have arisen along the way, one of the greatest being doubt and disillusionment. Countless times I have felt the sting of desiring the Lord and not experienced any response on His part. Such a double dose of pain has been mine as I have yearned for God deeply, and added to that pain has been a feeling of rejection or remoteness. With this twofold sting comes the immediate pull toward doubt that always becomes disillusionment over time. We doubt the Lord. We question whether He truly fills the hungry as He promised. We doubt ourselves. When we see no breakthrough, no tangible answer, we assume rejection and think perhaps the Lord has overlooked us and does not answer us due to our failings. When yielded to, these doubts become an immediate soil for the weeds of disillusionment to take root. This is where many sincere hearts—hearts that truly love and long for Jesus—give up in their pursuit of hungering after the Lord, painfully resorting to living at a distance from the One they love most.

One of the most costly aspects of love is the raw heart, open and vulnerable in a place of waiting and remaining unanswered. When we really hunger after God, giving our heart so vulnerably and expectantly to the longing, and contending for God's fullness in either our personal prayer life or in our circumstances, we know *true* pain and suffering of soul. Remaining in that struggle, even when seemingly yet unanswered, cannot happen by sheer willpower but by our receiving *revelation* of Jesus and His purpose for this age.

The revelation that must grow in our hearts is that Jesus is a Bridegroom who has betrothed us to Himself and made covenant with us (Matt. 26:27–29; 2 Cor. 11:2). Just as He told us, He has gone away for a time to prepare a place for us, giving us His Spirit as our guarantee, and He *will* come again just as He promised (John 14:1–3; 2 Cor. 5:4–6). Even now He sits at the Father's right hand, making intercession continually. He has not resorted to some eternal, distant bliss, living in far-off indifference from us. Rather, He continually watches and searches out our every moment, our every word, thought and deed, desiring that we would join Him in the place of yearning and hastening the day of His second coming (2 Pet. 3:12). This revelation of Jesus as He is even now keeps our hearts from their bent toward doubting Him. We understand that we are, in fact, *joining* Him.

As for the purpose of this age, we can be certain that part of it is to bring about this very yearning within the hearts of Jesus' Betrothed—even unto full maturity. Paul says that right now we are in this "tent"—our earthly body—groaning so that mortality might be swallowed up by life, for while we are at home in this body we are absent from the Lord (2 Cor. 5:4–7). The delay we find ourselves living in was never promised to be easy, and His call to us to hunger and thirst for Him was not designed to be comfortable, or soon satisfied. So often, when we feel that biting hunger for God, we make our prayer that He would somehow comfort us out of this longing. And yet, we have forgotten that, perhaps, many times He would wish the opposite. We want Him to comfort us out of the missing when, all the while, the missing is the very thing He wants us to experience.

In the place of prayer and longing for God, when we begin to feel somewhat rejected and denied in the long waiting, He might say to us, "Have I not told you that this life was a pilgrimage and these days would be those of mourning and longing for Me? Every wound that you endure for love will be jeweled with everlasting reward in the age to come. But now are the days of the aching heart, the weeping and the longing. In the midst of that mourning, do not distance your heart in your pain, presuming that I have distanced Mine. Do not forge self-protecting walls from your feelings of remoteness. Know and believe that your every word is heard deeply, your every prayer counted precious, your every tear kept forever (Ps. 56:8; Song 4:9; 1 Pet. 3:12). Remain in the longing and think not another time of My distance or aloofness, for I know no such capacity in My being. If My heart was so torn by the taunting of the masses when I walked the earth, how will it go unaffected by the sweetness of your hunger and affections for Me here and now?"

Hungering over Decades

In my own journey, the Lord has convicted my heart countless times of this precious gift called *longing* and of how He desires that I would actually live in undisguised hunger at the heart level, not just for a season, but over decades. Truly, this is a hard pill to swallow. For it is one thing to feel hungry for a time, and quite another thing entirely to remain in that place over a lifetime. Yet He calls us to bear the difficulty of longing without pacifying it, without distancing our hearts—not just for a few days or months, but for the whole course of our days.

Oh, that the statement of Jesus over our individual lives would be, "He misses Me, truly. She longs wholly for Me." That He would turn to His Father and say, "Father, there is one who misses Me." And that this missing would not be one of simply desiring an experience or a revelation so as to somehow have our cake of easy spiritual living and eat it too by receiving experiences of Jesus all the while. Rather, that it would be a missing ultimately unsatisfied until at last we are with Him and He with us. Experiences granted in this life and revelations given are only to strengthen our love for Him, thus strengthening us to live blamelessly before Him and expanding our longing for fullness until the day we see Him (1 Cor. 13:12; 1 Thess. 5:23).

Are we willing to *miss Him well* in our youth, at the cost of early promotions, at the risk of favor among men and success by their standards? Are we willing to remain in the vulnerability of hunger at the heart level in our thirties and forties, continuing in the way of love even when disillusionment comes knocking on our door and the visions of the early days seem too extravagant and too extreme? What about when the options set in, the responsibilities arise, the children come, and the cares increase? Will we fight for the simplicity of loving Jesus radically and press against the torrential wave that carries away so many over the course of the years? When decades turn and years accumulate, will our lives be such that Jesus would say over even our later years that love found its victory in us, and the steady tide of love became a mighty wave that no longer needed prodding but swept us effortlessly in its strength? Oh, that love would abound and win over us, burning within us in such a way that it does not diminish over decades but only steadily increases, until the day we see His face.

Glorious and incessant hunger in the human heart is one of the things that Jesus sought to lay hold of and draw forth with strength when He came in the flesh and walked among us. It is seeing Him that engenders an unrelenting yearning for Him. Thus, when He walked among us as a man and revealed to us the beauty of the incarnate God, manifesting and making known the Father and revealing the deepest heart of the Lord, He, in essence, was offering each human heart the most powerful cords that draw us to Him (Hos. 11:4; John 17:26; 1 John 1:2). He sought to lay hold of our passions and become the possessor of our every yearning by laying bare the wonders and beauty of the Lord before our eyes and hearts (John 1:14; 6:35; 1 John 1:1). Every moment of His first coming must become to us as a precious escort into increasing affection and thirst for Him.

Chapter Four

Beholding the One We Long For

Longing for Jesus only comes to fullness when it is contextualized between His first and second comings. Why? Because *beholding* and *experiencing* Him awaken our hearts to yearn for Him to return. Prior to Jesus' first coming, many yearned and longed for the promised Messiah. Anna's and Simeon's lives embodied this desire. Yet theirs was a very different sort of groan than that which laid hold of all who believed in Jesus and loved Him after He finally came (Luke 2:25–38). The difference between the two lies simply in the increased fervency of longing that comes with the increased knowledge of Him. The apostles and early church demonstrated with their lives the way that knowing Jesus in His first coming propels the heart into craving His return. As those who can say with John that we have beheld His glory, we are actually given the grace not only to long for Jesus in the provoking way that Anna and Simeon did, but to go beyond them in aching because we have actually seen and heard so much more (John 1:14). As John Piper appeals, "We know the Savior a hundred times better than Anna did . . . Shall we long for Him less than Anna longed for Him?" (84). Before His birth, they longed for a Messiah whom they had not seen. Since His death and resurrection, we long for a Bridegroom King whom we have beheld, known, and loved.

We must live with our hearts stretched out between both comings. For if we are only connected to His first coming, then we live out our lives extracting spiritual principles from Jesus' teachings and seeking to model our days according to His example. We cut short the story, closing our ears and eyes to the great culmination, and, in so doing, disregard the *person* who binds the two eras together. On the other hand, if we only remain connected to His second coming, our hearts have no tangible substance to lay hold of. We have no living face to love and long for, no person on whom to set our gaze or call to mind in remembrance.

We are bound to these two ages by the singular bond of the person of Jesus, the One to whom we are joined. He came the first time. He died, and He rose again. And He is alive forevermore. Shall we heed His words from His first coming and then refuse our hearts the joy and hope of the fulfillment of the story? Or shall we give great attention to the return of the Bridegroom, only to neglect to let our hearts be moved by every word He spoke to us, every loving touch He bestowed, and every kindness He conveyed at His first appearing? The first coming invokes a yearning for Him to come back; the second coming anchors our hearts in assurance that He will bring to completion what He inaugurated in the New Covenant when He came the first time (Jer. 31:31–33; Ezek. 36:26; Matt. 26:26–28).

We only know *who* is returning because He came once

before. We only know what He is like because He made Himself so clearly known to us when He lived among us. We only know just what kind of King He will be and just what sort of kingdom He will rule because we have seen His ways so vividly. Therefore, the only way to yearn for His return in fullness, with the substance of true longing, is to deeply engage through loving meditation on every moment of His thirty-three years of earthly life.

Beholding Him in His First Coming

When the Word became flesh and walked among us, it was as though the day dawned in the middle of the night and we could see who God truly was for the first time (2 Cor. 4:6). He revealed in every word and action what God thinks, what God feels, what God says. Part of His coming was to invoke our passion for Him. He came so that we would see and know the heart of God and that, in knowing, a true heart would emerge—the heart of an espoused Bride who yearns and ultimately cries out for Him in unity with the Holy Spirit just prior to His return (Rev. 22:17).

When we touch the person of Christ as He walked among us in the flesh, we do not touch someone neutral. When we encounter the real person of Jesus, our hearts are changed. We experience true kindness, true mercy, and true love, and we are never the same. Jesus came, and He opened up the revelation of God to us. In Him, we see who God is and what God says— what His eyes look like as He considers another, what His voice sounds like when He holds a conversation with a friend, what He feels and thinks, and how His heart is moved by the broken, the poor, and the weak.

By giving ourselves to loving meditation on Jesus, fully revealed in His first coming, our hearts will be moved to say, "I must have Him back. I must have Him in fullness. I long for that Man *who is God* to come again to the earth and to establish His kingdom." We are unable to initiate or fabricate mourning for the Bridegroom, as we have discussed already. But when we receive His touch, it is effortless.

We cannot be too familiar with the glories revealed about the heart of God when Jesus walked among us, revelations that usher us into the longing for Him that He desired. And so, we should consider three occasions from His earthly life, beginning with the tender manger moments, then the compassion displayed throughout His life, and finally the overwhelming passion of His cross. We will see how every event pulsates with profound revelation and truth, producing love in the heart.

Tenderized by His Birth

As a babe in a manger, He came to tenderize our hearts. The Child has much to speak to lowly hearts, much to convey to hungry souls and to any who will heed so tiny a voice. Have we become so familiar with the nativity story that we have relegated it to the narrative we tell our children in the Christmas season? And in so doing, have we neglected the gift of His nearness that the Holy Spirit desires to give to us through it— softening our hearts by it and piercing through our darkened understandings with the light of His nature there revealed?

The One we thought too far and too distant, too aloof and too indifferent to be known now lies before us as a Baby, so accessible. The One who created all things is now so close and approachable, having come to us in the form of a helpless baby.

We see who God is in His humility, in His meekness, in His gentleness. As we join the story and kneel with the shepherds to gaze in upon the One in the manger, our hearts and minds are confronted with the truth that this tiny frame before us is the Word of God, God in the flesh, and that He has come near to us for the sake of love. When God the Creator—the Covenant Keeper, and the Redeemer—lies before us in the form of a newborn babe, the effect in our hearts is explosive.

As we kneel beside the shepherds and peer into the cave, our hearts pounding with the weight of the angels' proclamation, we find Him there with wordless words, speaking so many things: "You thought I was too far and too distant, too aloof and too indifferent to be known. You thought that you were too weak or too broken to be received by Me. But behold, I am here in this dingy cave—I, the One who created all things. I am here so close to you in this cold night, inviting you to come near to Me."

Our wrong paradigms of the Lord are exposed to the truth of the One we thought was unapproachable, who now comes to us in the form of a defenseless baby. And the question must be asked: would we ever fear that a newborn baby might not want us near or think Him to be rejecting us? Would we ever wonder if He would rather another be in His presence instead? No! Without hesitation or the smallest inkling of rejection, we would hold Him fast in love and treasure the honor and beauty of such an opportunity. Babies do not reject another, and who would not rush into the privilege of holding so accessible a human frame? This is what Jesus whispers to us about His nature from of old in the fragile vulnerability of His infancy.

He is as approachable and embraceable as a newborn

babe, and His reception of us without rejection is as sure as a receiving infant in one's arms. Here in Bethlehem's stable, as we gaze upon the glory of God revealed in His face, He conveys mysteries that have been obscured since the foundations of the world, now revealed in brightest light by the Incarnate Son—mysteries about His humility, His meekness, His mercy. And as we gaze upon Immanuel now with us, our hearts become assured of His unchanging love, His tenderness toward us, and His constant receiving of our love given back to Him.

Even from these first moments of His infancy, our only fitting response is to gaze with trembling tears and let our hearts be washed by waves of so scandalous and glorious a truth: that this One is *God,* and *this* is what God is like. As we ponder how close He allows us to come, how He does not shun our presence or shield Himself from our love and worship of Him, our hearts cry out to Him, "Oh, who are we to be so near to You? And yet you desire us to come even nearer in heart and love. O, Christ Child, so tender, You have so many things to tell us and so many truths to convince us of. We wait here before You on this silent night and allow Your wordless speech to pierce our hearts over and over and over again."

Of these breathtaking moments in Bethlehem, Stephen Venable reflects so profoundly:

> Many scenes in the life of Jesus arrest the imagination but few as forcefully as the nativity of our Lord. To the redeemed soul the picture of Joseph and his betrothed huddled in a cave with a crying newborn becomes overwhelming. Their mean and lowly estate is seen

as grand, their weakness incites trembling.
Pressed to its bounds, the mind at last surren-
ders to the enormity of its beauty. While words
may compel one to kneel beside the manger in
adoration, only speechless love may pick up the
Babe and feel the immeasurable weight of His
tiny frame (20).

In this small and lowly frame, we find the confrontation
of God in all His merciful grace and kindheartedness, pleading with the human heart to approach Him and to part with
our accusations that say He is distant and far, detached and
disinterested in us. He invites us to embrace Him as He is—a
God of highest humility, approachability, and solidarity with
the ones least esteemed in the earth. Right here in this Bethlehem hush, our hearts are pierced by the wound of missing this
One, of longing to approach Him even as the shepherds once
did. We wish that our own eyes could gaze upon His welcom-
ing countenance, and be struck by the wonder of His tender
openness of heart toward us.

Marked by the Compassion of His Life

From the vulnerability and tenderness of the nativity scene,
we watch as Jesus lived out His life among men—so resolutely
expressing with His words, demonstrating with His actions,
and revealing with His responses what God is truly like. In
the same way that our hearts are struck by the condescension
of God in the Baby in the manger, we must allow our hearts
to respond to the One who was God in the flesh—walking
among us in the prime of His life. We must remember pre-
cisely who He was and where He had come from. He was not

just a prophet with a message or a teacher presenting a moral code. He was not just a healer or a perfect man. He was *God*—Yahweh incarnate—the One whose goings forth were from everlasting, and the One who created all things (Mic. 5:2; Col. 1:16–17). And everything about Him, in word and deed, expressed that identity. Beholding Him in this light brings us into the whirlwind and crosscurrents of His selfless act of humility and, in so doing, awakens love and longing within us.

One of the first things that should strike us as we consider Jesus as God in the flesh, walking among us, is His unwavering acceptance of men, though they rejected Him. Though He was God and the One worthy of all worship and adoration, the prophets tell us that He was the most despised and rejected of all men, humble in His appearance, yet not esteemed by men (Isa. 53:3; Matt. 13:57; Luke 4:28–29). He walked among us as a Man so lowly, so reduced, so lacking in the so-called dignity of self-honor. Jesus knew rejection from men deeply, from the day of His birth in Bethlehem to the moment of His death at Calvary (Luke 17:25). He experienced more contempt from humanity in His thirty-three years of life on earth than any other man before or since (1 Pet. 2:4). He was God the Creator who formed man for fellowship, now walking among us, and yet He was despised and rejected time after time.

The most potent part of this deep rejection lies in His response to it. In the moments when the crowds reviled Him, or the leaders around Him laughed in mockery, imagine the disciples' perplexity as they watched His implausible responses. When Peter and John would have made pride their ally by speaking condescending words to the scornful mockers, Jesus was silent. When they expected Him to ward off the rejection by rallying others against the ridiculers, Jesus instead refused to use His strength to belittle another. When they would have assumed that Jesus would turn from the ones rejecting Him and, at the very least, distance His heart in coldness from them, His heart remained, startlingly, in the nearness of love and far from the aloofness of conceit. Though He had every right to demand worship and reject those who rejected Him, He did not. He had no vendetta toward men, but baffled His resisters and His friends with His longsuffering (Matt. 9:35–37; 27:14; Luke 13:34).

These were the memories and moments seared upon the hearts of all who beheld and knew Jesus as He walked among us. And it wasn't just that He showed such amazing kindness and openness to those who ridiculed Him. All who knew Him saw a Man of surprising tenderness and graciousness, patience with the immature, and compassion for the weakness of men. His words, though piercing, were unlike any words ever spoken in that they lacked the sting of shame or the pain of rejection (Luke 4:22; 9:55). His eyes of deepest kindness penetrated to the core of their hearts, discerning their ways from the inside out. Yet even in full knowledge of every hidden motive and every stain of sin, such searching and knowing did not come with accusation or disdain. This One who knew all things loved them deeply and unreservedly. Though His jealousy was fierce over each one of them, He did not express it with displeasure or aggravation but with patient longsuffering and tenacious compassion.

Jesus continually reached for the weakest and the poorest ones, pulling them near and embracing them (Matt. 19:13–15; Luke 7:37; 8:48, 54; 18:16). Though He was the high and lofty One from everlasting, every cry of every child pierced His heart. God's own nature from eternity was put on display by Christ Jesus His Son. His heart responds continually to us even now as He is seated upon the throne of heaven. We can know with confidence that even the faintest prayers of our faltering hearts do not escape Him. Never could we rightly accuse Him of indifference, for Love can never be such, but is always concerned, always compassionate, always open and vulnerable—even at high risk and great cost. The One who called Himself "gentle and lowly in heart" cannot distance Himself from a single prayer of the poor widow, the lost son, or the broken sinner. The affliction of the afflicted wounds Him deeply. If He could be deaf to such prayers or hardened to such cries, He would invalidate His own law of love—He would compromise His very nature.

Consider again that our God does not use pride or arrogance to *shield* Himself from the hearts of men, as we so often do. In His perfection, free from conceit, instead of drawing back from others in self-protection, keeping His heart removed in indifference, He remains with heart open and engaged. Such unwavering vulnerability of the heart of God towards man finds its greatest impact as we consider His tender receiving of our every prayer, our every word, and our every action toward Him and toward others (Matt. 8:10; 26:13).

This Man, so familiar with suffering and so encumbered with compassion, challenges me with His incapacity for coldness or lack of concern. Always, He remains tender and open with heart exposed, just as it was when He pulled the adulterous woman from the dirt and showed her that her accusers had gone, just as it was when He stretched out His hand and touched the leper, just as it was when He allowed His friend John to lean upon Him and inquire of Him (Matt. 8:3; John 8:1–11; 13:25).

In finding this God face to face, we encounter the only One who is wholly *other than*. Our hearts cry out, "I never knew kindness until I knew You. I never knew love until I knew Jesus. I never knew mercy until I found it in You." Out of this revelation of the beauty of Jesus and the tender compassion He conveyed as God in the flesh, a longing for Him so natural and so inevitable arises from our hearts. Such a longsuffering heart brings our own hearts into a deep yearning for Him. We are overwhelmed with the desire to come under His gaze and behold the eyes of such tenderness that the crowds beheld with wonder. We desire that we might experience His holy affections—the love that left so many pierced to the depths of their heart.

Gripped by Love through His Death

Finally, Jesus invokes our hearts to love Him and long for Him by the passion of His cross, the penultimate picture of love for all time. For centuries, the cross of Christ has been the most precious meditation of the saints, and the myrrh of His sufferings has been the powerful fragrance lingering longest in the heart that considers Him.

We must behold Him there, hanging upon the cross—the Holy One, so bright in His sinless state, yet so reviled in His brokenness. Upon Him, we must rest our gaze. Here we find the pinnacle portrait of Love's most telling hour, the highpoint of Love's declaration, the picture that speaks a thousand times ten thousand words, etched deeply upon the pages of eternity, forever to be told. This was the day God displayed His love through the trembling thunder and scandalous story of *God crucified*.

As we behold Him here, the inescapable question that will rise from our hearts will be, "O, Jesus, what have You done in Your dying for me?" We are the poor ones, the sinful and the dark. We are those joined to the wretchedness of our self-absorption, self-exaltation, and self-love. And this One whom we gaze upon is He who dwells in the pure freedom of self-denial, self-abandonment, and self-sacrifice—the only One of His kind. What kind of jealousy burned within His holy heart? What kind of fury for sin and selfishness did He possess that He would submit to such shameful sufferings?

The cross of Christ's love tells the story so unflinchingly—the story of His extravagant love for man and His excessive hatred for sin—the twofold vehemence that ripped open the heavens with the sending of God's own Son. His love, like a potent stream flowing forth from this holy scene, called "Calvary," strikes our hearts like arrows as we consider it. It is the love that was so zealous in its fury against strangling sin that it sacrificed *all* for the saving of the soul.

This reality alone holds the power to pry our fingers from every other love. Gazing with loving and speechless adoration upon this greatest portrayal of love displayed is the secret of the saint in dying to self. The crucified life—the carrying of one's cross, the dying to flesh—is only found in the realm of love for this One who first loved, the One who laid down His life for His friends. It is in gazing upon the precious cross, falling in love with the One called the Lamb of God—our eternal Bridegroom—that we begin to draw upon the *power* of the love poured forth. This alone births love of its own kind.

Considering His passion is the place of light and truth, the place where shadows flee and the light of truth prevails. The sacred sketch of His sufferings in the meditation of the heart generates renewed certainty in His tenderness and confidence in the magnitude of His compassion and His affections so personal. It is not an old subject to revisit. It is a sacred mystery ever new that will keep us in trembling love for the duration of the eternal ages.

There is no greater meditation, no safer place to set the eyes of our hearts, than beneath the shadow of those sacred wooden beams, our eyes fixed upon the broken body of the One who is Himself God. He is the only One who ever truly loved us. Every drop of blood that drips down shouts a deafening song of love untold. Every glance into the most marred holy face wrenches our hearts into a heaving of at last believing that *it is true, all is true.* Oh, kindest God, it is true. No shadow of darkness prevails here. No arrogant accusation touches us in this place. No persuasive sneer dares a single word. Assurance upon assurance comes. We are loved to the uttermost. Here, hovering in the most holy silhouette of all time, we are kept most safe and we can finally agree with the words so bold:

> There is therefore now no condemnation to those who are in Christ Jesus . . . If God is for us, who can be against us? He who did not spare His own Son, but delivered Him up for us all, how shall He not with Him freely give us all things? Who shall bring a charge against God's elect? It is God who justifies. Who is he who condemns? It is Christ who died, and furthermore is also

risen, who is even at the right hand of God, who also makes intercession for us. Who shall separate us from the love of Christ . . . For I am persuaded that neither death nor life, nor angels nor principalities nor powers, nor things present nor things to come, nor height nor depth, nor any other created thing, shall be able to separate us from the love of God which is in Christ Jesus our Lord. (Rom. 8)

When we see the Man Christ Jesus who is God crucified, our hearts come into a holy boldness and confidence, and we cry out, "What shall separate me from that love, from the love of Christ?" Here is Love incarnate and Love defined. Here is God among us stretching out His arms and putting His heart on display. So shocking is this sacred sacrament that it rises high above the voice of the enemy and stands as our greatest truth, our sure anchor in the storm. Whenever our hearts fail us, our emotions revolt in torrent within, or the enemy assails us with lies of our being undeserving or disqualified, we run swiftly to this safest Shadow. There we gaze resolutely upon Him, until only Truth remains. Oh, beautiful sight, that leaves our hearts so torn, that grips our souls so fiercely, that leaves our eyes as streams and our hearts defenseless to believe. *It is true; all is true.* Oh, kindest God, it is true.

Of the cross of Christ, John of Avila cried out to the Lord:

> Great thief of hearts, the strength of your love
> has broken even our hard hearts. You inflamed
> the whole world with your love. Wisest Lord,
> inebriate our hearts with this wine, burn them

with this fire, pierce them with this arrow of your love. This, your cross, is indeed a crossbow that pierces hearts. Let the whole world know that my heart is stricken. Sweetest love, what have you done? You have come to heal me, and you have wounded me. You have come to teach me, and you have made me like someone mad. O wisest madness, may I never live without you. Lord, everything that I see on the cross invites me to love: the wood, the form, the wounds in your body; and above all, your love invites me to love you and never forget you (Liguori 9).

Having Seen Him, We Miss Him

The Lord invokes our hearts to love Him by the radical love, tenderness, and compassion He so perfectly and purposefully put on display before us in His incarnation. Each moment of His earthly life holds a drawing power to bring us into His heart. Each word He spoke becomes for us a window into the heart of God, and every action He performed speaks volumes to any ear willing to hear or eye eager to behold. Like a light in the middle of our darkness, He came to say, "This is who I am. Gaze until at last you believe."

How slow the human heart is to receive and believe the truth of God embodied in Jesus! We give lip service so easily to His graciousness and kindness, yet when this declaration is put to the test, how quickly do the doubts take precedence in our skeptical hearts. In fact, we have many inward barriers of resistance to such unthinkable kindness, as though our hands were continually upheld to Jesus in self-protection, saying, in essence, "You are *not* that kind. You are *not* that good. You are *not* that tender. You are *not* that gracious." Yet He will not allow our hearts to remain in this place.

In His infinite jealousy, Jesus will see to it that our circumstances and seasons provide countless opportunities for us to run up against these strongholds of the mind, until we at last come into the true knowledge of God. He directs our lives with great care so that we will finally believe Him, not just on the surface but in the deepest places of our hearts. When this happens, love takes root and becomes for us a torrent of yearning.

Mankind has never beheld One so trustworthy—One who would use His strength and power not for His own gain but for the lifting up of others (Phil. 2:6–8). Truly, He stands so utterly alone in His unequaled kindness and compassion, and in His matchless humility in using His power to lift up the weak (1 Sam. 2:8; Isa. 42:3–4). When we discover Him for who He really is, we eagerly desire that He would return once more, not just to lead our own lives, but to lead and establish justice in every city and nation of the earth (Ps. 72:4; 1 Cor. 1:7; Phil. 3:20).

This is the One for whom the disciples yearned. Longing for His presence, they were willing to do anything, laboring in order that He might return and establish His kingdom on earth (Acts 14:22; 2 Tim. 4:18; 2 Pet. 1:11; Rev. 11:15). And so, we, in turn, long and cry out with all of our hearts for Him to come again as King of the nations.

As we journey back, as it were, through these key occasions in Christ's earthly life, we find that as we behold Him, we are changed. Continually meditating on the words and actions of

Jesus' first coming, we position our hearts to receive renewed revelation of the person of God by His Holy Spirit. As our minds are transformed by the truth of His personality, His nature, His kindness, and His love, we find that the Lord's call to hunger after Him, long for Him, and mourn for the fullness He has promised is not only something He wants for us because it is *wise* to live in such a way; it is also because *we have been fashioned* to live this way. He beckons us to live in the only way we function rightly—thirsting after Him and finding satisfaction in Him alone.

Chapter Five

Thirsting for Him

Jesus sat alone at the well of Jacob, wearied from traveling on foot since early morning, hot and thirsty under the relentless beating of the noonday sun. Coming from the nearby village, a Samaritan woman approached the well to draw her daily water supply, undoubtedly lowering her eyes and quickening her pace as she caught sight of this solitary Jewish man positioned in her path. Having no intention of speaking or engaging with this man—as such a conversation would be unthinkable in view of the hostile culture between Jews and Samaritans—she quickly and mechanically began to draw water from the well, anxious to be done with her duty and flee such an awkward encounter. Suddenly, Jesus broke the silence, along with all of the common codes of culture, and said, "Give Me a drink." Stunned by His forthrightness, she asked why He, as a Jew, would do such a thing, since she was a Samaritan. Jesus answered that if she knew who He truly was, she would be asking *Him* for living water. Opening the secret of the ages unto her, He told her of the fading nature and inherent insufficiency of this earthly water to quench a thirst that is only satisfied with the unquenchable waters of Life (John 4:4–26).

In this conversation at the well, Jesus' words, timeless in their authority and power, address each one of us. We all—each human heart without exception—have spent our days and our energy drawing water from wells that offer the drink of only momentary thirst-quenching. We are admittedly thirsty, undeniably searching, and yet continually dissatisfied by that which we drink to slake our thirst. Yet even this does not alert us to the vanity of our well-dipping. Though unsatisfied again and again, we return incessantly for another try, another effort to relieve our longing. We go back to the cisterns of yesterday only to drink from them again today, faintly hoping that this time they will have something within them to satisfy our desire.

Thirsts in the Flesh

Whether we realize it or not, each one of us, by nature of our design by God, is *a living thirst*. As Thomas Dubay has coined the phrase, we are "incarnate thirsts"—thirsts in the flesh—"an aching need for the infinite" (*Evidential Power* 17). This is true of believer and unbeliever alike, and no man can avoid this condition. Every day, each one of us yearns out of an innate void within, a cavern undeniable that is thirsty for communion with God and unfulfilled by anything less. We were fashioned with this innate reach toward an infinite God with a very real plan.

Before the foundations of the world, before the age of time and the creation of the earth and of mankind, I imagine the Holy Three—the Trinity—in Their life and fellowship together

(John 1:1). Through holy imagination, I envision the divine counsel of the Godhead—Father, Son, and Holy Spirit—as They determined the future of mankind according to perfect wisdom and perfect will. Somewhere in this perfection of understanding, it was determined and ordained that every human heart would be formed as a living thirst—that we would be an ache, a groaning—pilgrims wandering in a world that is not our home. They made us for something greater and *Someone* greater, for another kingdom with the only true King.

I imagine in the eternal counsels it was decided: "Let them be thirsts in the flesh." And I envision the Son stepping forward and saying, "And *I* will be the *living water*. I will be the only One who can ultimately satisfy." And so it was.

Man was formed around an internal cavern that would set him apart from all the rest of created order. While the hamster is content to run his wheel, mankind forever remains discontent with the horizons he has already beheld, forever on a quest for the next great gusto and satisfaction. In a word, he is thirsty for something *beyond* him, for man was made for the Infinite. Man was made for God.

Though this ache resides in the deepest parts of each human person, it does not belong to her in the sense that she might choose to extinguish it or live without it. To the proud heart who does not love God, this could not be more offensive. For no matter how hard she might try to escape it, she cannot be independent of the Lord and cannot escape her undeniable need for God. This cavern—so to speak—was there before ever she discovered it, and the only one that has rights to it is the One who called it into existence in the first place.

Endless Ache for God

Think about the best day of your life—the day when everything was going right and all the circumstances were thriving, relationships and favor with others were soaring, and finances were plentiful. In this context, Dubay once more pegs the human heart in its challenging corner when he proposes that even in the seeming perfection of your most ideal day, no matter how apparently great the circumstances, if you were really honest when your head hit the pillow at the end of that day, you would find yourself asking the question, "Is that *it*? Is that *all* there is?" ("Thirst for God").

The psalmist rightly cries out, "O God, You are my God . . . my soul thirsts for You; My flesh longs for You in a dry and thirsty land where there is no water" (Ps. 63:1). We walk this land, wandering in a world that offers no fulfillment. We can be answered only by the infinite One. Even in the perfect set of circumstances and life situations, when everything by secular standards would be considered ideal, the groan within remains untouched and unpacified. We were not made for perfect circumstances but for a perfect Person.

Describing the way in which Jesus answers the human heart with Himself, the Lord once said to a young woman named Angela of Foligno, "Make yourself a capacity, and I will make Myself a torrent" (Dubay, *Deep Conversion* 74). Here we hear the Lord's promise to us and His instruction as to what to do with our hunger. He desires that we would be as a space opened and outstretched toward the divine—Himself. In *jealousy* He wanted us for Himself and refused to give over our ultimate satisfactions to anyone or anything else. We are to turn our innate thirst like a yawning cavern and direct it with a heart of faith and love toward God, refusing to fill this open space with lesser frivolities and waiting like a dry cavern for a divine deluge to come soon.

This recognition and embracing of our need are my glory and yours. This God-given and God-answered ache on the inside is our great possession as pilgrims awaiting our final destination. We are living thirsts because He is truly living water. We were made poor and needy very purposely, hungry and vacant very deliberately. The One who formed our frame and fashioned our souls for Himself wrote the script in such a way that only the soul that says yes to this thirst and goes on a quest for the infinite will ever experience sustained satisfaction. Simply stated, if we do not find lasting pleasure in Him, we will not find it. And we must recall again that this is what makes our thirst so precious. It is not a mark of deficiency in our being but a sign of being truly alive. The hungriest people are those most alive, and those most connected to their great need are those closest to touching what it means to truly live.

God desires to give Himself completely to us. He desires our hearts to flow like a river on the inside (John 4:14). However, we must first make ourselves a capacity in order to be filled. This is how we cooperate with the divine and partner with His hand. He will not force His way upon our lives. He waits to be wanted. He lingers in His answer until longing arises. And it is only out of this place of embracing our innate dependence and looking to Jesus as our only source that we are prepared for the posture of heart necessary to live as friends of the Bridegroom who mourn for Him and yearn for His coming.

Turning Need into Encounter

I used to hear words of Jesus such as, "Those who are well have no need of a physician, but those who are sick" (Luke 5:31), or "Blessed are you poor, for yours is the kingdom of God" (Luke 6:20), and think, *How kind Jesus is that He comes to the lowly and meets the poor. How compassionate He is that He comes to the sick ones and does not despise or neglect them in their condition.* Without realizing it, I missed the whole point. It isn't that Jesus is so compassionate that He gives blessing to the poor, to the sick, or to the hungry. When He spoke these things, He wasn't saying, "And I will *even* remember the poor and the desperate." No, each of these words conveys the only door of entrance into knowing and encountering Christ.

He was not saying, "And if you happen to be sick, I'll heal you. If you happen to be hungry, I'll feed you. If you happen to lack wisdom, I'll give it to you." In actuality, He was pleading with the human heart: "Will you recognize your deep-rooted poverty and come to Me? Will you admit to your pervading disease and sickness and come to the only One who can heal? Will you admit your utter foolishness and come to Me as the only source of wisdom? Are you willing to accept the true deficiency of your condition and come to Me for the answer?"

Jesus has made the heart-posture of poverty and desperate pursuit central to the Christian life and indispensable to the journey of loving God. The gospel of Jesus begins with a blessing to those who are thirsty, to those who are unsatisfied and found wanting. The entryway to knowing Him begins with acknowledging and embracing our own poverty, rather than forever seeking to somehow rise above this human condition.

Jesus pronounces a blessing on those who embrace something already possessed by every person if they will but recognize it—poverty. This isn't to say that we who are spiritually thirsty are living the gospel. The fact is, we are closer to the truth than those who do not recognize their own lack. The blessing comes to those who perceive and embrace the thirst, undergoing the humility necessary to admit that they have no answer in themselves and are utterly dependent on a Source outside of themselves.

We will never be given an option as to *if* we will thirst. Our innate yearning for the Infinite is as inescapable as the body's need for water. Yet what we do with that thirst belongs to the mysterious environs of the free will. We do not voluntarily thirst, but we do voluntarily turn and direct our thirsts toward the Lord. To hunger and thirst for righteousness is altogether different from simply hungering and thirsting. All are created thirsty, but only he who directs that ache for years on end towards the Lord, towards the person of Christ—refusing to commit himself into the hands of the smothering hosts of easy satisfactions and temporal enchantments—only this one is guaranteed to be abundantly satisfied.

The Lord will take even the smallest thirst that we offer Him and do something so striking with it. We offer up to Him our tiniest aches, and He receives them as precious and valuable, over time causing them to increase and expand. When He has His way and we continue to yield our longing unto Him, what began as a whisper of desire eventually takes over our hearts, ultimately possessing us and wholly winning us over. How often my heart is moved by this kind exchange of the Lord. I give Him only my little longing, and over time He turns that ache and that wound into a torrent of affection so strong I am left with no other option but to be riveted with every passion upon Him alone.

The Test within Our Thirst

Here we are, with a vast, gaping need outstretched, and there is only one *narrow way* of satisfaction—the person of Christ. Our great challenge in the Christian life—and especially as Christians in the Western world—is that we must *experientially know* Jesus in a way that answers our need at the deepest level. Pretenders of passion are quickly exposed when challenged by the trials and disillusionment of time. If we can only repeat ideas about Jesus, we will fall into one of the greatest traps set by the enemy. We will think we have pursued Him and found Him *lacking* when in fact we never actually *found* Him to begin with. If we do not touch the person of Christ in a profoundly intimate way, we are in danger of reaching the place where we either yield to the deception of dullness, or even worse, turn from Him utterly at the heart level and claim Him to be insufficient or inadequate in fully answering our deepest cravings.

This is where every man becomes prey to the world's enticements. The enemy has no trouble with men and women who claim love for Jesus but live lives that prove their affections to be right here, in this age and in all of its comforts and values (Isa. 29:13). He makes his aim elsewhere—at the heart of the one willing to live in the tension of painful yearning for Jesus and continued resistance to the deceptive pull of the cares of this life and the spirit of the age.

We must not be unaware of the target we become to the

hosts of darkness when we give ourselves to a radical thirsting and longing for Jesus. How rare are the ones who live continually open to the Lord in the place of longing. How few are they who, having tasted of Him and aching increasingly for fullness, embrace the wound of love in a daily way and refuse to settle for the alluring comforts of this life. Upon these, the enemy sets his attention and his aim.

Yet this should not keep us from full givenness to such hungering after God. Saints throughout history have considered it joy to be an object of offense and a focus of attack for the sake of Christ, and the Lord will give grace to such as these. At the end of the day, we are left with the question: do we really have the option if we truly love Him and have known His perfect love? When such profound encounter with Jesus has transpired, we do not ask questions or entertain hesitations about loving Him radically, even at high risk. Love has already conquered and consumed in its path all of our *so-called* options of yesterday. We have been marked and ruined by Him, and now, for the sake of love, we must declare His worth even with our thirst.

Witnesses of His Worth

As we progressively find Jesus to be indescribable fulfillment and delight, we have only started to achieve the purpose of God in fashioning us with such a thirst. Once more, the question before us in our day as we live in between the two advents of Jesus is: what is He looking for? It is about Him—His worth and His inheritance in us. First, it is about our fellowship with Him in the place of mourning, joining with Him in the very groans of His heart. And second, it is about a witness going forth across the earth, that, to the dilemma of the human person, there truly is an undeniable answer. Part of our role as friends of the Bridegroom is to be those who give witness and testimony to the worth of Christ by the desire and longing that characterizes our lives.

And here is where we, as those who love and adore Jesus, move from simply thirsting because we were fashioned that way, to actually thirsting and longing out of the place of relationship. We have tasted of and known Jesus, and our thirst is the direct overflow of this. In a world that is spinning endlessly around the hamster's wheel of unfulfilling and empty pleasures, there comes a sound entirely foreign and unknown. It is not the rise-and-fall sound of someone finding a momentary delight only to be suddenly silenced by the inborn insufficiency and fleeting nature of that pleasure. Rather, it is the sound of a steadily growing momentum of deep, unquenchable delight.

Out of humanity's fray of disillusioned hearts, shattered dreams, and jaded hopes arises a testimony wholly distinct and rare. It is the testimony of a heart that has come across true treasure—the very treasure for which every human longing was formed and from which every wanting originated. The voice of this testimony does not diminish or grow old, but becomes a progressively increasing declaration of the beauty and worth of Jesus. This witness cannot be imitated, cannot be forced, and cannot be faked. When one has touched the living God in the person of Christ, he has finally found the fountain of living waters (Jer. 2:13; 17:13). Such a singular sound arises in stark contrast to the deceiving claims and assertions of this world's fleeting passions. While every other cistern is eventually found to be dried up and empty, this well of living water arises as a steady stream, surging forth in undeniable declaration of the everlasting and unrelenting rivers of abundant life in Jesus.

Truly, we must fight to preserve this precious thirst by aiming all of our affections on Jesus. Yet again, such centralized focus and narrowed passion is what Satan most despises. He will do all that he can to keep us from living in such a way. One of his choice strategies to deceive us in the place of thirsting and longing for Jesus is simply to allure us into an ever-so-gradual and cunning dullness that smothers and threatens to snuff out the precious fires of heart-hunger within. He stretches out this line of attack over years and even decades, for if this dullness took over suddenly, he would not have such a high success rate. We must prepare and make ready for such assaults of darkness, that we might not be fooled and deceived by his subtle current that sweeps so many into its path.

CHAPTER SIX

Fighting Dullness of Heart

Perhaps the greatest foe of true mourning for the Bridegroom comes with the deception of constantly filling the incessant void within us with temporal and secondary things that will never satisfy the hunger and never satiate our thirst. These secondary things are not always wrong in and of themselves, yet the effects of using them in the wrong way are dangerous.

Filling ourselves with these inferior pleasures day after day will lead to our demise if we do not change our ways. We dull the very ache that is our glory and muffle the cry that is to be the song of our pilgrimage, the song that keeps our hearts alert and in love in the midst of wartime. We spend each day clouding our hearts with a thousand numbing distractions. We stuff our souls with countless comforts that one by one silence and stifle the groan for God. This groan was intended to resound with clarity and purity, cutting through the fog of this present age and all its delusion.

Stifled Souls

The human heart in its fallen state says that discomfort is damaging and thus wrong. We so easily come to the place where we no longer feel hunger for God; we no longer yearn or groan or ache for eternity because we are inundated with the cares of this life and the comforts of this age. This is the crisis that happens so frequently in the Christian life—the crisis of spiritual dullness. One begins in fervency and, without even recognizing it, begins to suffer greatly at its hand.

Just as Jesus sat before the woman at the well, He sits before each one us without exception, desiring to bring an end to our incessant drinking from broken cisterns (Jer. 2:13). I think specifically of believers in the western world who "know Him" yet still find themselves thirsting after all the inferior delights to answer a craving that they have yet to find in Him. He peers into our very souls, searching, with the eyes that see all and know all, for some fraction of hunger not yet choked by earthly pleasures. He seeks some faint thirst still unquenched and unexhausted by the torrent of temporal delights.

Jesus will only give Himself to the hungry. He will only pour water into a thirsty soul. He waits to be wanted. But we do not realize we are full beyond measure, satiated beyond our realization by a thousand distractions—whether they are mental, relational, occupational, or simply amusing. We do not know how quenched our souls are, and yet the demand of the kingdom of God, the prerequisite for encounter, is always hunger and thirst.

How I feel the pleading eyes of Jesus here in my own heart and life. Each day, I have so many opportunities to come to Him to quench my thirst or to resort to one of the multitude of distractions and numbing options all around. These occasions come as I am pressed in many ways, by both the smallest discomforts and the truly painful times where circumstances leave me anxious or distressed. Many of the things I might reach for in these times are not wrong in and of themselves. The ache within, however, was not meant for them; nor will it be answered in them. It was meant to cause me to "grope for Him" (Acts 17:27).

To turn to these lesser fulfillments in these times leaves me in a worse place than before because of their deadening effects upon my heart. To resort to them instead of simply turning my heart to Jesus shifts me further into dreaded dullness, if not actually deadness that requires at least an awakening, if not an outright resurrection. And here, Jesus' eyes beckon me deeply to see every possible difficulty as a moment to cry out to Him, to allow discomfort to strengthen my reach for Him, and in so doing to cleave to Him still more. Dullness of heart does not *have* to grow in our lives, yet if we do not consciously seize each moment and each dilemma with a response of love and obedience unto Jesus, the inevitable does transpire.

The Crisis of Spiritual Dullness

One of the first spiritual crises in the Christian life is that of spiritual barrenness. Here we recognize how much we lack in God, how great our need for Him is, and how little we possess in the true knowing of His heart.

A second spiritual crisis comes later in the journey, perhaps after several years have passed of walking closely with the Lord. This is the crisis of spiritual dullness caused by the mundane and the familiar. It is a testing of the first things, a trying of that which the Lord first wrote upon our hearts after having gone deep in the message of His extravagant love.

The first crisis of spiritual barrenness is portrayed in the Song of Solomon when the maiden realizes that her own garden she has not kept; her own heart she has neglected (1:6). Our response to this crisis is an inward awakening that leads to a headlong pursuit into the deep things of God. It's a leaving behind of the former ways and a wholehearted embrace of the beauties and affections of His heart. Everything is new and fresh and alive, giving the human heart the holy thrill of what it was created for—encounter with God's extravagant love. We begin the journey with the understanding that we are dark yet lovely, yet even in our darkness and weakness, God embraces us (Song 1:5). When this truth is discovered for the first time, nothing could be more powerful and transforming to our hearts. We begin to truly live as we reach out of our barrenness to the fullness of His love, finally being answered in the deepest cravings of our hearts (Ps. 36:8; John 15:11; Eph. 3:18–19).

In the second crisis—that of spiritual dullness—the fervency that once fueled our course has lessened. The new language that once thrilled us is new no longer, and the novel ideas that revolutionized our hearts at one time are now the common lingo of our everyday experience, the ordinary and unexciting. The high vision we once held and promises we once believed now seem a bit of a stretch and perhaps somewhat farfetched. Herein lies the test. When the human heart grows weary with the well-known and bored with the common, it begins to grow inwardly distant from the things that in years past it called most precious, including the Lord Himself. The distance is most often unperceived.

When we have lived long in the realities of His affections and tenderness toward us, we fight the tendency to not feel the same strength of gratitude or wonder as we did at first. This is the warning signal of our need to be most careful in the guarding of our hearts and the preserving of the tenderness that we once knew. As portrayed in the Song of Solomon, the little foxes begin to nip at the vines, and if not dealt with, they will cut off the life flow in due time (2:15). Without a strong pursuit in the other direction, the heart will be taken by this pulling current of dullness, even growing to despise the language, the message, and the rhetoric of what was so dear in the early years. Within this strong pull, we can lose our way in what lies behind the language—the very realities that set the heart free and bring all joy and satisfaction in God (Eph. 5:15–16; 2 Thess. 3:13).

Adding to the tensions of this dilemma is the disappointment that comes with the years of encountering our weakness time and time again and so often falling short. We began with the leap of faith that God could actually be *so* extravagant in His love, but now comes the need for a greater faith—that His mercy truly *endures* and that the simplicity of His extravagance cannot be overshadowed by even the longest lists of failures. We grow weary of presuming upon His mercy and receiving His embrace amid failures. Over time, our own weariness with our weakness brings the subtle distance on the inside that will eventually destroy the heart, if it is allowed to remain.

This most certain trial is a crossroads that cannot be avoided and must be faced head-on in order to avert the sure slipping away into an attitude of coldness and hardness—or even worse, deadness—of heart. Jesus referred to it with severity when He described the time before His return. He said the love of many would grow cold (Matt. 24:12). Thus, it is a dilemma not to be treated lightly. The way that we remain steadfast in the difficulty of this crisis is to continually keep our eyes and hearts upon the person of Christ and remain in the gaze that began the process of love (1 John 2:24).

Peter tells us that in order to not fall from steadfastness, we must *grow* in the grace and knowledge of our Lord and Savior, Jesus Christ (2 Pet. 3:18). We must not lose the continual communion and exchanges of love that are most precious in this life (2 Tim. 1:14). It is a time to go yet deeper still in the mysteries of His love, in trembling before His Word, and in fear of Him. We must dive below this crossroads, not yielding to the pull of cynicism so strong, and refuse to succumb to the attitudes of indifference and disdain.

Deep in humility, we must receive His affections at a greater level than ever before, with all gratitude that He has known our path, has seen every pitfall and every stumbling block, and has set our feet in a safe place. With a heart lifted up by a faith stronger than it was at first, we must lay hold of His eternal mercies and let the truth about Him be written upon our hearts in a way that only a long history in God can inscribe. We must cleave to hope in the Lord yet again, knowing that it will not disappoint, that it is sure and steadfast, and that we do not hope in vain (Rom. 5:5; Heb. 6:19). In responding this way, the test will serve to *further* our depth in God and will intensify our gratitude, our testimony of His mercy, and our assurance of His continual embrace. It will lead us not away from Him but closer to Him. We will find Him and, embracing Him, vow to never let Him go (Song 3:4).

Fighting Disillusionment with Future Hope

Still another colossal contributor to spiritual dullness of heart is the stronghold of disillusionment that arises out of the affliction of delayed answers and unfulfilled hopes. "Hope deferred makes the heart sick" (Prov. 13:12). Time and time again, a formerly young and boisterous heart sits upon the sidelines, jadedly convinced it must have been wrong to once have believed and hoped so fervently. Assuming itself to finally be swallowing the necessary pill of reality, it chooses to give up believing. This crisis has turned many a believer, once so fervent, into the pain of disenfranchisement and disappointment in their latter years. It is a dangerous place for the heart to slip into, and such a crisis calls for a determination to take hold of truth rather than retreating under the weight of disappointment. It is a time to renew our minds according to His Word, counting and confessing it as our highest truth (Rom. 12:2). When what we have believed according to His Word does not match what we have seen and experienced, we must resist the compulsion to accuse and doubt the Lord.

Without question, one of the reasons disappointment, and even offense, moves in upon us at such rapid speed is that, without realizing it, we have planted our hopes in the soil of the *present* far more than we realize. The writers of the New Testament unapologetically pointed toward the day of Jesus' return as the place where our hope—the dream of our hearts—is to be anchored and set (1 Pet. 1:13).

The hope of our lives—that driving force and motivation which inspires us to persist through trouble and fills our vision for the future—is most often tied to something we see in the realm of earthly circumstances. We set it in this present age rather than solely in the appearing of Jesus and the age to come. Because of this, when circumstances do not play out as we planned, when our lives do not unfold as we dreamed, rather than our hearts reaching for the comfort in the certainty of our beloved King and Bridegroom's appearing, we feel let down by the Lord and grow disheartened. We then distance ourselves from Him.

In my own pursuit of the Lord, I have found myself in this crisis many times. After crying out to Jesus in the place of longing, believing Him for a greater encounter and tasting of His nearness or sensing a true breakthrough of His power, my heart has sunk into the silence following. It has come under the tide of disillusionment at His seeming distance from my prayer and my expectant soul. Many times, when I have found myself in this pattern of letdown—where I have opened my heart in longing and found no answer, or cried to Him in prayer and heard no response—the Lord has shed light and opened my eyes to see that part of the reason for this disappointment was tied to my hopes being set in the wrong place. Rather than resting my hope in the future—as an anchor set fully upon the ultimate consummation to come at Jesus' return—my hope was resting in the here and now and the breakthrough I would see today (1 Pet. 1:13).

If given words, my perspective in these times might have been something like, "Yes, I know that Jesus is coming again and that day will be awesome. But what I am after is the full measure that He would give me today." Now, at a moment's glance, that sounds like a seemingly sound perspective. After all, we are to contend with great zeal for the fullness that the Lord would reveal to us here and now. Yet, ever so subtly, something truly has been amiss in my heart in these times. And the slightly off part was the order in which my hopes were anchored. First, I was hoping and setting all of my focus upon the present breakthrough. Second, and at a distance, I was holding Jesus' return as my point of hope. Both of these were right pursuits but should have been kept in the reverse sequence.

As I would leave a time of longing prayer feeling nothing in my heart—or leave a time of contending for breakthrough in intercession and see no change in circumstance—my heart would feel despair. I would even begin sensing an offense toward the Lord. To my surprise, instead of the Lord remedying these jaded hopes with quick answers in the present, He has over and over lifted my eyes to the future and the promise of His coming. In times like these, He has seemed to say to my heart, "Your focus must rest upon My return and the grace to be brought in that day so as to keep your heart from offense in the present delays" (Phil. 1:10).

We are in the tension of the present and the future. Without question, we must continually ask the Lord with faith and expectancy for the *now*, contending with urgency for every fullness He will give in the present day, both in personally knowing Him and experiencing Him, *and* in the breakthrough of circumstances in physical healing, finances, relationships, and the like. We contend for our own personal lives and for the lives of others. Contending with faith for the full measure of all that He would give right now is vital to our lives and commanded by the Lord. It is grounded in God's desire that we would ask in His name, and that He promises to answer our prayers (Matt. 7:7–11; 21:22; Mark 11:24; Col. 1:23; Jude 20).

Jesus taught us to pray always and to not lose heart in the

process (Luke 18:1–8). Yet our anchor of hope is not fixed in the present answer but in the future day (Heb. 6:19). This is the hope that we rejoice in, the hope that purifies our hearts along the way (Rom. 5:2; 12:11; 1 John 3:3). And how are we kept in persistent prayer and continual asking without losing heart? Not by mastering a certain endurance level, but by holding fast to the ultimate dream of our heart that is sure and steadfast, immovable and certain. And the blessed hope is of Jesus' glorious appearing (Titus 2:13).

When, therefore, the delay happens and we do not see what we had expected, our response should not be one of despair and feeling rejected. We should purpose to rest confidently in the promises of the Lord and in the surety of their fulfillment. Just as the heroes of the faith in the book of Hebrews continued in faith without wavering, not having received the promises yet being assured of them, we are invited to set our hope fully ahead (Heb. 11:13). The Lord invokes us, in this fight against weariness and discouragement in our souls to look unto Jesus, "the author and finisher of our faith." and, by setting our eyes on Him fully, to overcome every hindering weight of offense and disheartenment (Heb. 12:2). This is how we are beckoned by the Lord to ward off the force of spiritual dullness brought by disillusionment and weariness and to run with endurance the race set before us (Heb. 12:1). When we make *this* our hope—the glory to come at His appearing—we are not disappointed because, with this hope, the Holy Spirit pours out love into our hearts (Rom. 5:5).

Fighting to Remain Awake

The human heart, who can know it? Who can search it

out? Having depths indiscernible and secrets unperceivable, it winds its way down a thousand trails, harboring mysteries of unnumbered proportions and keeping a man as far from knowing himself as a baby born into the world, unfamiliar with its surroundings and unable to discern his own person from that of any other. It is in these hidden chambers of the human heart—these imperceptible pockets—that the enemy wants to keep even the redeemed heart asleep, under the deception of dullness and unaware of its own condition. He does not wage war against us blatantly but subtly, causing the sleep that we fall under to go unnoticed and the dullness to go undetected. This is our great dilemma and a severe obstacle—to be overcome slowly day in and day out. We are asleep, and we must be awakened. We are dull, and we must be sharpened. We are dead, and we must be resurrected. And only by first recognizing the danger zone that we live in will we become revived from this state.

Our reality is that we must be kept awake or else we will most certainly sleep. Whether we realize it or not, we are up against a constant current that is unrelenting in its strength and gives no leeway in its persistence. Hearts are unaware as it sweeps them into its possession; only in purposed resistance can its snare be avoided (Rom. 13:11; 1 Cor. 15:34; Eph. 5:13–15). Peter warned:

> Beloved, I now write to you this second epistle
> (in both of which I stir up your pure minds by
> way of reminder), that you may be mindful of
> the words which were spoken before by the holy
> prophets, and of the commandment of us, the
> apostles of the Lord and Savior, knowing this

first: that scoffers will come in the last days,
walking according to their own lusts, and saying, "Where is the promise of His coming?" For
since the fathers fell asleep, all things continue
as they were from the beginning of creation.
(2 Pet. 3:1–5)

We do not realize how greatly influenced we are by the
scoffing spirit of our culture and the age in which we live. The
residue of this spirit clutters our thinking and our fervency,
leaving us unknowingly dulled. We live under an incredible fog
while we think our skies are clear.

The globe has been lured to sleep under the "peace, peace"
hypnotization of the evil age, and even those who are saved
have been influenced by its seduction. When the Lord shakes
everything that can be shaken, the fault lines will be uncovered,
and the dormant things revealed (Heb. 12:27). As the crescen-
do of human history builds at the end of the age, the earth,
including our very hearts, will be saturated in this seduction
and sleep. Things are not right, and we do not know it. In fact,
things are desperately wrong, and we hardly notice. The world
is under the sway of the evil one, weighed down with darkness
and wickedness, and many believing hearts have grown cold in
their love for Jesus (Matt. 24:12).

When our hearts deceive us and the world holds sway over
our affections in a way that such a disruptive burning ceases
in its sting, then it is time for us to stir up and strengthen that
which remains. We must beseech Him to remove our blinders
that dull us. Once more, it is deep connection to Jesus and the
hope of His return that severs our worldly ties. We must behold His glory, His beauty, His power, and His kingdom until

our affections for Christ burn brightly once again and our ache for Him overtakes our apathy (Titus 2:12–14).

Christ will not return without such a groan. Our role to play in this day and in this hour is certain. And it will cost us everything to really carry it out. We must be friends of the Bridegroom. We must be those who eagerly await His appearing and live in perpetual longing for the day that is our blessed hope and our great consolation. We must tear our hearts in a humility that recognizes our own lack of love for Him, our own distance from such groaning. We cannot be satisfied with the state of things as they are. We cannot be busied with earthly ambitions and plans alone. We cannot allow past offenses or disillusionments to define our way ahead. We must set aside our ambitions for our own lives, our hopes that are hinging upon our own pleasure rather than on Christ Himself. We must throw ourselves with abandonment into lives that are consumed solely with Jesus and His return.

To be sure, the eyes of Jesus engage each one of us so personally in this fight against dullness. He knows the hordes of darkness that rail against our hearts, luring us into the caves of disenchantment and dashed hopes. Yet even in this difficulty and in this fight, He pleads with us out of our own history of having known and experienced His love and His goodness. He urges us to set our eyes in the right place—upon Him alone and His most glorious coming. It is *love* once more that provides the power to choose rightly in these times. And the good news is that He helps us in this wrestling, not leaving us empty-handed. It's as though Jesus would say, "Yes, you are up against something great. Yet My Father and I have determined a lifestyle—a way of posturing your heart out of the motivation of love and desire for Me—that will strengthen your pursuit of Me and reinforce your fight against subtle deceptions of the spirit of this age. It is a lifestyle not fueled by human willpower but by the force of *desire*. And it begins not in strength but in voluntary weakness."

CHAPTER SEVEN

Mourning in Fasting

Fasting hardly strikes us as something affiliated with desire and the longings of the heart. Instead, we think of it as a challenging discipline charged by strong will or bodily restraint. We think of it as a spiritual practice reserved for times of crisis and tragedy when we cry out to God for a breakthrough in some area of our lives. Yet God's plan for fasting moves far beyond this. Jesus placed this exercise right in the center of love and described it as an expression crucial to longing when He responded to John the Baptist's inquiring disciples. In chapter one, I mentioned Jesus' rhetorical question: "Can the friends of the bridegroom mourn as long as the bridegroom is with them? But the days will come when the bridegroom will be taken away from them, and then they will fast" (Matt. 9:15).

With this statement, Jesus reclaimed the gift of fasting for one of its primary functions as a fueling agent of love for God and as an arouser of aching for His return. With these words spoken first to John's disciples, but so relevant to our own hearts and lives, He pointed us to a time when He, the

Bridegroom, would be taken away. During this time, fasting would take on the face of enhancing and sharpening love and longing in the lives of His friends. We would fast because we miss Him and want to be given to a lifestyle that expresses and makes manifest that ache.

One of the ways that we stay fervent in continual longing for Jesus, warding off the spirit of slumber that seeks to steal our fervency and preserving a heart that misses Him, is through this *desire-motivated* fasting. This expression of our mourning for Jesus is one of God's greatest secrets given to strengthen our love and our endurance along our journey of faith in this age. In the plethora of so many comforts and satisfactions at our fingertips, the least we can do for our hearts is set them in the solitude of fasting before God alone as an act and a statement that He is our true treasure. This commands our affections into a unified stream toward the One we so love, while at the same time refusing the divisions of heart that so subtly subvert our sole passion for Him alone. There is no secret power in fasting in and of itself. It is when fasting is matched with love in the human heart, serving as a strengthener of godly desires, that one of its highest purposes is realized.

Drawing on thoughts from *The Rewards of Fasting,* a book I coauthored on how we express our mourning for Jesus through fasting, we will see how such a lifestyle begins with longing, transpires in weakness, and lasts but for the moment of this age (Bickle, Candler).

Born in Longing

This type of fasting is born in longing and thus moves beyond fasting for immediate breakthrough in circumstance. It stretches for breakthrough in the heart, both in the *now* as we grow in love and satisfaction of the Bridegroom, and ultimately in the longed-for day of supreme breakthrough—when He returns for us. In a fast so rooted in desire for God, we fast not to achieve God's attention but to touch Him once more, to experience Him in a deeper way, and to know Him at a greater level. We fast not simply to express our ache, but to enhance it, causing our missing of Him to increase and multiply.

It has always been the case with those in love that when they are faint with love, food is far from thought. When the heart is sick with desire, the body and its natural needs silently surrender to their secondary position. Such is the case with our relationship with Jesus and the fasting we give ourselves to in the context of that relationship. We fast as an overflow of the love and longing of our hearts to be near Him. It is a fast motivated by desire and sustained by longing, a longing for Jesus that arises to such a severe degree that food in the natural becomes a lesser priority, as the heart-craving for Jesus supersedes all else. This is the kind of mourning Jesus described. He says in essence, "After tasting of My love, after experiencing My kindness, after touching the depth of My tenderness, you will find no inward toleration for My absence. In those days, you will not fast out of duty but out of the heart-wrenching ache of love for Me."

It is true; there is a mourning that can only be awakened in separation. How can we mourn when He is present with us, face to face and eye to eye? These are the days of rejoicing and celebration, when longing sleeps and the ache is answered. Jesus described His friends as not needing to fast when the Bridegroom was with them—in the days of His earthly life—

for fasting is unnecessary when the longing for His nearness is fulfilled by His immediate presence. Those are days of drinking in His every word and every deed. Yet, oh, how different is the case when the Beloved is away, in these days in which we presently live. Right before the wedding, the Bridegroom departed, leaving us with the forceful, inward pounding that repeatedly asserts, "Things are not all right. Things are not all right. Things are not all right—until He comes back." Once more, love mourns in absence, and fasting, in the way Jesus spoke of in this passage, is again fitting.

As I have embraced this sort of fasting through the years, with my motivation being desire to know Him more and the longing for my own heart to live in tenderness and yearning for His return, how I have come to cherish this gift. Without question, I have known *many* times in fasting that were mostly difficult and uneventful, but the fruit of the years of such mourning for the Bridegroom who is away right now has helped to awaken my heart in a greater measure. Truly, I am not the same person as I once was. My love for Jesus is not the same; neither are my desires in life the same. And these changes were not brought about by severe discipline, but by deep tenderizing of a dull heart; not by my somehow moving and convincing God to do something in my life because of my heroic self-control, but as the tiny flame of my desire for Jesus was fanned and fueled through the grace of fasting.

To fast in this way is to agree with the way that the Lord made us from the very beginning. Fasting says, "I was made for more! I will not settle into the dullness of the secondary when I could be alive in the piercing thirst for the Infinite. I could be quenched by the raging torrent of the divine!" We fast the *secondary* so that we might be answered by the *primary*. We set aside our inferior pleasures so that we might wait for the fulfillment that can only occur in the *superior* pleasures of God. We leave behind our faint desires for Him that we might be brought into the impassioned heart of love that will not relent in its force.

Just as the Lord spoke once to Angela of Foligno that if she would make herself a capacity, He would make Himself a torrent (Dubay, *Deep Conversion* 74), He has invited each of us in the same way. We make ourselves a living capacity awaiting a greater experience of the infilling of the Spirit, and in so doing, we enter into our glory as those who were made for God. In time, the ache escorts us into the torrents of the living water Himself.

He is bringing forth a Bride throughout the earth who loves and yearns for Him, voluntarily choosing Him in the face of every evil. A deep mourning must be awakened in the heart of the ones betrothed to Him. We fast to remind our hearts that He has been taken away, for we have grown used to His absence. The fasting gives way to mourning, and, in mourning, we enter the holy cry, "Come!"—the cry that all of Scripture presses to leave in our hearts.

An Invitation to Weakness

Fasting is about weakness, and even the first mention of it in the gospels gives invitation to a lifestyle of desperate leaning upon the Lord. In His teaching that would become popularized later as the Sermon on the Mount, Jesus spoke unparalleled words about the kingdom of God—words that would change human history forever. He spoke of fasting in the realm of food, time, and giving. We fast our natural strength in fasting food; we fast our time by investing ourselves in prayer; we fast our financial strength by giving to others. Each is a way to volunteer our weakness in order to desperately lean into the strength of our Lord. To anyone who has ears to hear, Jesus was saying, "Listen, if you want to know Me, if you want to embrace Me, this is the lifestyle you will find Me in. If you have ears to hear and a heart to obey, this is how you, the one who desires friendship with Me, will live before Me." And perfectly and profoundly, He disclosed some of the most detailed descriptions of how to live and how to love in the way that God designed—in our perpetual humility of weakness (Matt. 5–7). God always chooses the weak things to shame the wise, and choosing voluntary weakness is the way we emulate the wisdom of Jesus in becoming poor or weak (1 Cor. 1:27).

Without argument, the nature of our pride despises the place of weakness. Putting on strength appeals to us. Choosing weakness and remaining there is simply counter to every natural inclination within us. Why did God choose fasting as such an important way to meet Him and to intensify spiritual reality? Why has He made something so simple—not eating and choosing to pray—so powerful? Natural hunger is a reminder that we are *not* self-sufficient but dependent on a wholly-other-than, sufficient One. Our natural hunger is a stark daily reminder that something outside of us must sustain us in order for us to live. Thus, giving ourselves to fasting means that we voluntarily give ourselves to this *glad dependence*.

The paradox of fasting is perplexing in that our natural weakness could actually serve to strengthen us in our spiritual lives. We embrace less strength in order to experience more of

God's power and presence. This happens when our physical weakness reminds us and convinces us of our overall need for the Lord, thus driving us to the place of prayer and fellowship with the Holy Spirit. This prayer and fellowship with God in turn strengthens us greatly with an undeniable inner fortitude.

God fashioned such a gift within the realm of fasting. Somehow, He designed us so that when we give ourselves voluntarily to this kind of weakness, with the motivation of growing in love for Him, our hearts actually expand to receive more of Him. This isn't because we earn it or because we do something to make the Lord respond to us. Rather, the fasting actually postures us to receive more deeply and profoundly the love and experience of God that He always desires us to know. We fast not to move God but to move our own hearts into His heart. And this simple heart-expander makes way for both a greater experience of intimacy with Jesus in the here and now, and a greater love and longing for Him and His soon return.

Inner Clanging and False Clinging

When we give ourselves to fasting and prayer, denying our flesh in the process, one thing we will quickly encounter is the intense inward clanging of protest. We have immediate inward resistance to any form of denial, and this conflict might be far more forceful than we were prepared for. The intensity of our wants and cravings is not revealed until they are denied. Fasting is one way to put the cravings of our flesh in check and allow our spirit to take dominance for a time. It both reveals and silences the roar and appetites of our natural man. Because of our culture in the West, we are apt to seek immediate pacification of every craving and desire. Because of this, when the inner clamoring arises, we quickly do whatever is necessary to stop the noise and silence the cravings so that we can get back to being ourselves again.

The reason for our inward revolt is that the inclinations we are voluntarily denying in fasting are that of self-sufficiency, self-reliance, self-indulgence, and self-focus. Such impulses of the soul do not like to be denied. As ones formed and fashioned for God alone, we refuse these compulsions so that we might enter the river of true delights. "Feeling good" and propping up our flesh with the comforts of this life—though they may even be good pleasures, given of God—is not our goal. Finding our pleasure and enjoyment in Jesus and casting all of our affections upon Him should be our ambition. Our goal is that every earthly pleasure and gift would serve to enhance and foster that holy center of gravity.

Fasting brings such an abrupt disclosure of just how much we rely upon false comforts. Hunger presses us into bodily discomfort and when we find ourselves uncomfortable, we reach for ways of escape. If we are fasting that which typically eases our discomfort, such as food or entertainment, the state of our soul is seen in its true light. In both our humanity and culture, we are prone to want things immediately and to miss the wisdom in waiting or the beauty of longing without an instant answer. What we do not often realize is that quick satisfaction does not promote longsuffering or the deepening of desire or love. We start to see these things as a crucial part of our progression in intimacy with God. The Lord loves the process of delaying His answer in order to bring about greater love in us.

Though food is a gift from God to be enjoyed in celebration of His kindness, His abundance, and His love, it has great potential to be a stumbling block if we reach for it to fill the inward ache that God alone can fill. This wrong sort of reaching and false addiction is what fasting exposes. And nobody likes to be exposed. In our natural man, we would live the rest of our lives propped up by innumerable stimulants other than the Lord and His Word. This is why the role of desire, that precious gift from God, is so necessary in fasting. It takes a great recognition of our spiritual barrenness and a deep yearning for Jesus to make us voluntarily position ourselves before God in prayer, fasting, and utter vulnerability, allowing His Holy Spirit to expose the ungodly addictions within. It takes a deep dissatisfaction in things as they are, accompanied by a swelling vision of eternity and the culmination of this grand story.

Only a deep longing for Jesus—both for our souls to be utterly alive in true intimacy with Him, and ultimately for His return to the earth—could convince us to willingly posture ourselves in voluntary fasting, undergoing the difficulty that accompanies this revealing of our flesh. Yet this is where love takes us. Thus, for the sake of love, we put ourselves voluntarily in this crucible. Our cry is for Him to search us and remove from our hearts and lives every hindrance to loving Him, until Jesus stands alone as our true portion and our sole affection.

Momentary Fasting

Our fasting, just as the longing that motivates it, is temporary. We fast for a moment, and then, for all the ages to come, we are satisfied with the One we love and have yearned for. Our fasting for the Bridegroom must be contextualized before this backdrop. We have but this one moment in the age of *faith*—the age where we see dimly—to love our Jesus with such strong hunger and to lavish upon Him the gift of our fasting-intensified yearnings. So our fasting is a momentary mourning, to be met with an *eternal* satisfaction and fulfillment in the person of Jesus and His everlasting kingdom.

Jesus' question, "Can the friends of the bridegroom mourn as long as the bridegroom is with them?" is fitting for the age to come, in as much as it was true for the days of His first coming. When He returns and the Bridegroom is again with us, we will fast no longer, but will live in the joys of His presence and the fellowship of His nearness. Thus, for all eternity to come, how precious to God and to our own hearts will be the ache and the mourning of these present days.

Intermingled with His tender institution of the Lord's Supper, Jesus Himself spoke of His own fasting until that future day when He said, "I will not drink of this fruit of the vine from now on until that day when I drink it new with you in My Father's kingdom," and "I will no longer eat of it until it is fulfilled in the kingdom of God" (Matt. 26:29; Luke 22:16). We recall again that our longing is always preceded by His, and even our fasting follows after His own.

In the ancient Jewish wedding tradition, the bride and groom would often fast on the day of their wedding, breaking their fast together afterward as part of the celebration of their new life as one. I believe that possibly part of what Jesus revealed in His own abstinence from this table until its fulfillment in the kingdom to come was the heart of our eternal Bridegroom. He came into the world as the Bridegroom, seeking to betroth His Bride to Himself. And having laid down His life as the price paid for her, He awaits the day when He will come a second time and receive her to Himself (John 14:3).

Though *we* will continue to partake of this communion table as a way of keeping our hearts in remembrance and hope, and as a way of strengthening our hearts for greater abandonment and loving sacrifice, He waits to eat it anew with us in the glorious kingdom to come. He awaits the day when the desire for which He prayed so fervently to His Father will be finally and fully realized. He anticipates the time when those who belong to Him from every tongue, tribe, and nation will be with Him where He is, beholding His glory forever and ever (John 17:24; Rev. 5:9–10). For this day of gladness He yearns, and in the same way—and for that same day—we also yearn (Song 3:11).

The marriage supper of the Lamb awaits us. How glorious will be the celebrating and the feasting together (Isa. 25:6; Rev. 19:9). With our Bridegroom, we yearn in these days. With our hearts and lives, our bodies, souls, and minds, we *long* in this age. For this brief moment of the age of faith, we do not withhold from the One we adore the full measure of our longing and fasting, knowing that for all eternity we will look upon it and treasure it as one of the sweetest gifts we have presented to Jesus (1 Cor. 13:12).

This lovesickness surrounds our hearts as a protective cloud in the hour of trouble. And in this place of mourning, we are free. Our cry arises: "Bind my body, close my mouth, take away my name, and you have not conquered me. I am heartsick with love with eyes into another world. You cannot touch what has been wholly given to Him, for He has set His seal upon my heart and locked me away in the freedom of holy love forever. My heart mourns a Bridegroom, and there is no mountain I would not climb, no sea I would not cross to be with Him, to meet His embrace."

Radical love has never fared well with those who have not tasted of Christ and found Him to be the most precious One, laden with unsearchable riches and glory (Eph. 3:8; 1 Pet. 1:7). Yet such abandonment to Jesus also sends forth a witness of something and Someone glorious to any who have ears to hear and eyes to see, appealing to the hungry with the fragrance of life rather than death (2 Cor. 2:16). Such rarity of devotion perplexes those caught in the sway of empty passions. To the one so riveted and compelled by love for Jesus, nothing makes more sense. It is our love for Jesus, our passion for His return, and our longing for His second advent that set us apart from the world and mark us as strangers and pilgrims in this life.

Chapter Eight

Living as Strangers

S trangers do not begin as strangers in a foreign place. They begin as those *from another home*—from a place familiar to them (Heb. 11:14). They cannot feel like foreigners among a set of companions unless they first have been friends of some company elsewhere.

The gnawing feeling so common and the inability to finally feel at rest leave the stranger far from home, forever secluded in his foreignness, though he may reside for years on end in this "away" state. Just ask anyone who has made his home in a foreign land. Such a feeling of remoteness comes upon the alien in a very natural way and manifests as homesickness. It is a feeling difficult to avoid and impossible to ignore. The over-riding emotion of homesickness infuses every day like a hidden fragrance, always having its pull upon the heart, never leaving it completely free to settle comfortably in a home somewhere else.

Severing Worldly Ties

What makes us pilgrims in this life does not hinge first

upon our separation from the world but upon our union to Jesus. Just as a foreigner is only such because he has a home elsewhere, we become separated from the world by virtue of first being joined to the person of Christ and being citizens of His future kingdom (1 Cor. 6:17; Phil. 3:20–21). When the Lord saved us as we looked upon Jesus and believed in Him, we were joined to Him as His Bride and as His Body—bone of His bone and flesh of His flesh (Rom. 7:4; Eph. 5:25–32). This, then, is the starting point to living as strangers in this world and in this life. Though once in friendship with the world, now we are separated from it by virtue of our union to Christ (1 John 5:4–5). As our fellowship and love for Jesus grow, and our life becomes increasingly centered on the coming day of His appearing and the age to come, so also are we separated from the world and its cares.

It is our union with Jesus that has ushered us into a deep knowledge of Him and an incessant longing for Him. Now, by virtue of both our relationship to Jesus and the love that has compelled us within that relationship, we find ourselves in a wilderness, so to speak, in this age and in this world as we now know it (2 Cor. 5:14). Love has caused the separation. And our hearts being so caught up in Another. The One to whom we are both joined and betrothed has made us those who live with a continual sense of homesickness in our hearts, and those who the world does not recognize as its own.

Consequently we see that we are not strangers because we have willed it or because we have figured out how to conjure an external change; we are strangers not by mastering a method but by knowing a *Person*. Out of our union with Him comes a steady growth in love for Him, which becomes the force of forsaking the world and cleaving to Him. Our transformation from those once so at home in this world to those who grow increasingly strange to all our secular surroundings happens through His own life and love working within us, forging in us a holy awe and provoking a battle for righteousness as we look toward the day of His appearing (2 Tim. 1:12; Titus 2:13). We abide in Him continually, and, in so doing, we bear much fruit in conforming to His likeness (John 15:1–8). Our affections become powerfully set upon *somewhere else* and *Someone else*, marking us as peculiar and foreign to the world around us (1 Pet. 2:9–10).

The Forming of "Strangers"

The world first hated our Lord and, correspondingly, hates those who are His (John 15:18). The age in which we live is evil and corrupt. The whole world lies under the sway of the Evil One, and the Lord urges us through His Word to make no alliances and no friendship with it (Rom. 12:1–2; Jas. 4:4–5; 1 John 2:15–17; 5:19). Jesus is so starkly in opposition to the world, the spirit of this age, and the lusts of this life (John 1:4–5, 11). He is the One who has gone before us and invites us to be with Him where He is (John 17:24). Jesus said, "I am not of this world," and, in His own choosing of us out of the world, we have entered into this great paradox of being in the world but not of it (John 8:23; 15:19). By bringing us into the unequaled, glorious position of favor and fellowship with the Godhead, He has also brought us into His own animosity with darkness. He has made us enemies of evil, while clarifying that the world would surely hate us just as it hated Him, for we are not of the world, just as He is not (John 15:18; 17:14, 16).

To be *in the world but not of it* is a common phrase we hear in Christian circles, but it is no small assignment (John 15:19). Yet Jesus did not speak these words and this charge to us as some task to overcome in our own strength—how overwhelming the thought. When He came in the flesh and we beheld Him in His beauty and kindness and love, we were given the very means necessary to fulfill this call.

We must bear in mind that it is love that marks us and wounds us and does all the work of separation for us. For love, God has separated us unto Himself, and for love, we offer ourselves as living sacrifices, separated unto God (Rom. 12:1; Eph. 2:11–13). The One who saved us, made us His own, and who transforms us day by day, is the One in whom we have placed all of our treasure. Because our treasure rests in Him, our heart is with Him also (Matt. 6:21). Wherever our heart is, there we find our resting place. It's no wonder, then, that we ache, long, and yearn to be there. We become strangers to this world in direct correlation to the profound proximity we find with Jesus, the One we love. In as much as we are at home in Him, we are not at home in this world.

When He invites us to live as though this world is not our home, truly it is a call that we reach indirectly (Rom. 12:2; 1 John 2:15–17). We do not begin by making it our aim to grit our teeth and resist earthly pleasures or sinful appetites. We make it our aim to place all of our treasure, all of our hope, all of our dreams in Jesus—the One we love, the One we will marry, the One who will return and rule as King over all. Our ambition above all else is simply Jesus—to know Him, to love Him, to encounter Him, to become like Him, and to ultimately dwell with Him for all eternity. If this aim is in place and we truly begin to know Him in such a way, then we leave the realm of having to continually resist appetite after appetite by entering the freedom of embracing one all-consuming appetite, the desire for more of Jesus.

This treasure so marks us that the world and its honors and delights lose their pull upon our hearts. This radical reach for Jesus as our highest pleasure is far from passive, but is, in itself, an active resisting of the world, its pull, and all its fleshly lusts. We hem ourselves in and bring our flesh into subjection by putting on Jesus and surrounding ourselves with Him continually (Rom. 13:14; Gal. 5:16, 24).

As we have considered, it is neither a moral code nor a set of disciplines that we hold before us, but a Person. Jesus, with His eyes of piercing love and tender affection, is the One who calls us out of friendship with the world and into friendship with Himself. This One whom we love and are hidden in is unlike any other. He is the One most holy, most other-than, most beautiful—His very person is unsearchable riches (Eph. 3:8). And He is our Bridegroom who is so *jealous* over us. He does not want part of us, but all; not fractions, but the fullness of our hearts and lives (Matt. 22:37). His hatred for sin and for the swaying of our hearts toward any lesser thing is rooted in His absolute jealousy that we would be wholly His, without separation. It is knowing this heart and beholding these eyes that force us out of indifference and to flee all that divides us from Him.

Hastening His Day

To be a pilgrim in this life and only at home with the Lord—to love Him so radically that we become as those of whom the world is not worthy—is more than an option, more than an invitation, and more than a good goal (Heb. 11:38). It is part of the role we play in speeding His return (Acts 3:19–20; 2 Pet. 3:12). Recall to mind that our participation in bringing the One who sits at the right hand of the Father *out of heaven* involves living out the consecration of a betrothed Bride, awaiting and beckoning her Beloved's return just before the wedding day (2 Cor. 11:2).

It is not a passive role that we play as strangers in this world, simply waiting for the coming day and future age. Our role is supremely active with great ramifications. As those who live as strangers in this world, not conforming to its lusts, we are not only to look for and long for the day of Jesus' appearing, but also to hasten it and speed its coming (2 Pet. 3:12). The picture of the Church at Jesus' return is that of a mature, corporate Bride who has made herself ready for Him, dressed in the white linen of righteous deeds (Rev. 19:8). Thus, part of this hastening happens in conjunction with our choices for righteousness and our fight to be wholly His. Peter appealed to Jerusalem to repent so that times of refreshing would come and God would send Jesus back (Acts 3:19–20). How incredible the thought that we have been given the potential to either speed up His return by our lives of loving Him and walking blamelessly before Him, *or* slow it down by our compromise.

So how does one hasten or speed His coming? Hastening happens first, once again, through and as an outflow of our union with and love for Jesus. This love in turn empowers us to respond fully to Him without reserve and acts as the forceful escort to separate us from the world and its ways. Our passion for Jesus also compels us to selflessly do good works in

His name, urging many to glorify God as they witness these manifestations of our continual yearning for Christ and for His kingdom (1 Pet. 2:12; 2 Pet. 1:13–16). Jesus is returning to a Bride made ready, and that readiness comes to pass in conjunction with our choices of obedience and love. Thus, though we cannot know all the mysteries and all the variables in the grand scope of the Lord's leadership, God has made available to us the capability of accelerating His return.

Holy Wrestling

And here we must soberly wrestle with the state of things. For though we desire to walk in holy love and blamelessness, a wakeup call comes to us regarding the subtle aspects of compromise that we so easily embrace, the chief one being that we have found our home in a place other than Christ Himself. Though we might like to imagine we are living as the pilgrims His Word describes, being strangers toward the cares of this life and the spirit of the age that brings sleep to the earth, the truth would most probably surprise us. We have far more comfort in that which is far from God than we are aware of, and far less consolation in His own heart than we would dare imagine. And this is where we must hear His yearning and pleading heart to flee these comforts and compromises that we have grown so used to, for how awful the probability that we are more at home when He is far off than when He is near.

This possibility we must ponder and come face to face with, for by every natural inclination and propensity we are drawn to love darkness rather than light (John 3:19). And if *He* is the One who is strange to us, then that which is familiar is surely our foe disguised in friendly costume. If He who is our home is not our dwelling place, then without even realizing it, we have set up camp in enemy territory. Here the devourer destroys us one day at a time without ever having to so much as lift a finger in struggle against us.

This, then, is no small matter. Under the influence of the Evil One, the world and its enticements are far from harmless (1 John 5:19). The cares of this world, the deceitfulness of riches, and the desires for pleasures in this life powerfully entice us on every side (Matt. 6:25–33; Luke 12:13–21). We are in desperate need of an uprooting from one comfort zone to another, for we cannot serve two masters (Matt. 6:24). Preceding this uprooting, we must be awakened to the truth of our false comforts and alerted to the implications of such vanities.

Oh, how it wars against all that is natural to us to truly be strangers to this world, to refuse and reject the notion that we must settle in, that we must find comfort and find our place in this life. We wage this war each day like fighting against a raging storm that never abates. It is not an easy resistance or a one-time struggle, and without realizing it, we are often obliviously battered by this fierce storm and uprooted from our place in God. This is our struggle, our holy war. We fight not against flesh and blood, but against every evil of the ruler of darkness who would seek to overcome us in this way (Eph. 6:12).

This war that we wage is fought directly through the Holy Spirit within us, the living flame of love who destroys that which stands in opposition to all that is not of God. By our fellowship with Him, by the inward experience of His love and the deep penetration of His Word, our fellowship with darkness loses its power. Through communing with Him each day, we are brought increasingly into the place where Jesus dwells, and we depart more and more from the world that He deemed not His home. This is the secret of the stranger.

Truly, we cannot live any other way, as if there were several neutral options. To live outside these sacred boundary lines of wholehearted love is not to live at all, for it is in God alone and in loving Him fully that there is life. Any life outside of Him is but a fading flower, temporal and fleeting, a vapor at best.

We *cannot* live at home in this world. And if we do, something has gone desperately wrong and needs to be made right. But if we choose Him with all of our hearts, even in the face of trouble and lack of ease in this life, we will embrace the Lord's purpose of conforming us to His likeness. We will find ourselves in the crucible in which our love is made worthy of the Son. And the eyes of fire that search from heaven to find lives of faith and love in the hearts of His friends will see the beginnings of a love so holy and so radical—lives so filled with love and free from compromise that they fulfill the mandate to hasten the coming of the Lord (2 Pet. 3:12).

A Stranger's Consolation

Just as the Lord did not desire that we should struggle in our own efforts to leave the lusts of this life, He did not purpose that we would hold our breath in the realm of pleasure and delight and never touch it until the day we finally see Him. Quite the contrary, He described the fruit of our relationship with Him as having life and having it more abundantly (John 10:10). He longs to bring the human heart into fullness of joy (John 15:11).

The stranger is not one who is stripped of every pleasure. Rather, he is laden with unseen joys, which, though unseen, are not temporal, but eternal. In other words, He will not leave us on this pilgrimage to pine away in unanswered longing. The very way He keeps us sustained in our journey, the very power of our pursuit, is through true consolations that He entrusts to our hearts. He does not only give us *one* taste of His goodness and love, but many. The thirst that is quenched only in Him does not just become more parched until Jesus comes back, but is answered by the living water that alone satisfies, each and every day. The Holy Spirit wells up within us as an ever-flowing fountain, and rivers of living water flow abundantly from within (John 4:14; 7:38–39). There truly are real consolations to be known and real encounters with Him to be had, and to the one who makes himself a stranger to this world, God makes Himself the Beloved, so near (1 Cor. 2:12).

The portrait that God has given throughout His Word to illustrate His Self-giving to the one who has fled this world is that of the wilderness. As pictured by Hosea, He draws the one He loves into the wilderness, away from the entrapments and temptations of this enticing world, and He allures her to Himself in the dryness of the desert. There He speaks comfort to her heart and teaches her to sing (Hos. 2:14–15). He tenderizes her heart in this place and wins it over to Himself.

Part of our pursuit on this journey, as our hearts are set on pilgrimage, is to ask for and receive from the Lord's hand every gift and consolation, every breakthrough and encounter that He desires to give in the here and now. Our anchor of hope is fixed and set on the coming day. Thus, we do not despair in the days of dryness, imagining the Lord to be withholding His nearness from us.

As we look with faith toward our future expectation, we

know that every joy is coming and every consolation is certain. Yet at the same time, with this anchor in place, we cry out for every foretaste God will give of that coming day. For each time He speaks a word to us, we behold with greater understanding just what He is like. Each time we see His power made manifest in our day-to-day lives, we are strengthened with might on the inside to continue on with greater love, faith, and endurance (Eph. 3:16).

We want and need all He will impart to us in the experience of His heart and the swelling of love for Him in the present day. It would be a wrong and unbiblical perspective to think that we simply hold out until His coming without contending for the fullness that He would give to the human heart today. Part of our pilgrimage is the continual tasting of Jesus by encountering Him, the steady increase of knowledge, and the progressive deepening of love in our hearts as the path grows brighter and brighter before us until the perfect day (Prov. 4:18).

Fools for Love

Though strangers to this world and in this age, we are the furthest thing from being strangers to the Lord. He has made us alive together with Him, raising us up and making us sit together in the heavenly places in Him (Eph. 2:4–6). In His going, we have not been cut off from Him but joined to Him; we are in Him, and He is in us (John 14:20). Though aliens and pilgrims now, we are not alienated from Him, but, as those who are in Him, the whole of our lives and identities are with Him where He is. As stated previously, we are only strangers in the first place because He has joined Himself to us and we have found our home in Him.

How often in my own journey have I succumbed to the lie of alienation, assuming the Lord to be far from me and even stingy with His comforts and consolations. I have felt the pain of this age of the unseen. In that lack of full sight, I have postured my heart as one simply *surviving*, all the while imagining the Lord to be somewhat miserly and sparing with the pleasures He possesses in great abundance. I have often wrongly assumed that somehow I would flee all temporal pleasures only to find myself somehow disqualified from the pleasures in God for which I forsook all. Yet this is such a deception and stands in direct opposition to the true nature of God. His extravagant personality is far from stingy and His Self-giving so shockingly abundant. *He* is the One who has brought us into this wilderness. Will He not also be the One who comforts us with His nearness and causes us to sing there? Most assuredly, He will not forsake us, but will cause us to be more alive in the midst of this voluntary desert than had we all the resources of this transient world at our disposal.

When I find myself doubting this extravagant exchange, His eyes of gentle love pierce through my soul and beseech me to stop my spinning round and round, and to finally become conquered by His love that is unutterable in its heights of kindness. Will I go on imagining Him to be withholding His heart from me when, in truth, it is ever open to me as one hidden wholly in the beloved Son? Paul argues with my misconceptions: "He who did not spare His own Son, but delivered Him up for us all, how shall He not with Him also freely give us all things?" (Rom. 8:32). With such doubts, I forget that it is only by His gracious abundance and scandalous generosity that He has saved me and I have come to Him at all. The message of

His cross and His profuse and unmeasured love is so extreme that the world calls it foolishness. To all who receive it without resistance and without skepticism, it is the power of God and strength for living (1 Cor. 1:18).

In my walking as a stranger in this world, may I not make the mistake of thinking *God* a stranger to me by my doubting Him. I do not want to be a skeptic of God's love in even the remotest sense. In the midst of this age of faith, I would rather be a *fool* for love, spinning wildly and childishly through my days with every kind of presumption of just how grandiose His enjoyment, just how extravagant His delight in me, and just how excessive His Self-giving, than to stand on the sidelines with arms folded, waiting for the "real" rendition of His love, the "actual" account of the story.

As a child does not argue with his father or mother when they give him their hearts in a love indescribable, God invites us to receive His incomprehensible love. Oh, that we would be fools for love as we walk as strangers in this world, asking with confident hearts for every consolation He would give, every encounter with His wondrous love that He would impart. Instead of second-guessing the One whom our souls love, we should rush in with arms outspread—with speed and diligence that no *cynic* would employ—and we should know and believe the Love He has for us. Wisdom in this age is not to be modest in faith, hope, and love but is to be excessive and unhindered. May we be counted with the fools and strangers who believe beyond what is perceivable, who reach past what is tangible and visible to the unknown regions of the incomprehensible love of God, and find our home in the fellowship that is more real and more rewarding than any visible consolation, any temporal solace this world can offer (1 Cor. 4:10).

Loving Jesus and longing for Him, fasting in His absence, and craving His immediate presence have brought us to the other-worldly posture of heart that marks and wounds the friends of the Lord and the Bride of the Lamb. Our yearning has a true end and a final hour. We long until we see Him. We hunger until at last He comes to fully satisfy. We ache until our foretastes of Him transition into complete fulfillment. We mourn until we are with Him once more. Longing lasts but for a moment and is then swallowed up in a moment on *one* glorious day, the day on which we have set our eyes and fixed our hope—the day of Jesus' return.

CHAPTER NINE

Loving His Return

Jesus will not stay where He is in heaven forever. The One who came the first time, dwelt among us, died on our behalf, and then ascended to heaven to take His seat at the right hand of the Father is *returning* to the earth. When He ascended the first time, as the disciples were still looking into the sky, the angels spoke: "This same Jesus, who was taken up from you into heaven, will so come in like manner as you saw Him go into heaven" (Acts 1:11). This coming of Christ is not an elusive event or an ethereal moment but a tangible, concrete, *bodily* return of the One we love and adore. The *Lord Himself* shall "descend from heaven with a shout, with the voice of an archangel, and with the trumpet of God" (1 Thess. 4:16).

What began at the cross has yet to be consummated. The One who purchased our redemption the first time He came will come again to complete what He began (Heb. 9:27–28). He who sits at the right hand of the Father even now—the One who was taken from us up to heaven and the One to whom we are betrothed—has a day that burns continually before His eyes. The Bridegroom who stretched out His arms and allowed His precious blood to be spilled on behalf of the ones He loves, has a wedding day—the day of the gladness of His heart—before His eyes (Song 3:11). Long ago He promised that though He was going away to prepare a place for us, He would again return and receive us to Himself (John 14:2–3). Upon this day, He has set His jealous and holy gaze. He does not forget. What we so quickly lose sight of burns perpetually in His heart. He has not failed to keep this day continually before Him, and He will not relent until it comes. He *will* consummate what He started. There will be a wedding!

Loving His Return

In the days following Jesus' ascension, the friends of the Bridegroom, those who had known Him, walked with Him, loved Him, and adored Him, began to walk out this tension of living in a continual yearning and eager awaiting of Jesus' return. I imagine John turning to Peter and saying, "Peter, do you remember what He said to us on that last night before the cross? He said He was going away to prepare a place for us and that soon He would come again and receive us to Himself. He cried out to His Father His own desire that *we* would be with Him where He is, beholding His glory (John 14:2–3). Peter, He told us that He was the Bridegroom and that before the wedding day He would be delayed for a time (Matt. 25:5). Peter, *here we are.* He's ascended to the Father. He is no longer here in the flesh. Oh, I miss Him. Oh, I can't wait till He comes again. I long for that day with all my heart."

And Peter might have responded, "We truly are pilgrims and sojourners right now. *He* is our home. *He* is our life. All of our hopes are tied up and set fully upon Him and the grace to be brought to us in the day of His return. John, I can't wait. Everything in me reaches for Him in a continual *looking for* and *hastening* of that day" (1 Pet. 1:13; 2 Pet. 3:12).

Nothing could be more natural for the disciples and friends of Jesus than missing Him when He ascended to the Father. Nothing could be more instinctive than to yearn for His return and live in radical abandonment, as lives poured out in offering as an overflow of that longing. As we have considered, Jesus not only desired friends at His first coming; He wants friends *now*. He desires a lovesick Bride—a yearning Church—before His return. And He will not return without it. He has set His heart upon it, prophesied it, and jealously works within our hearts by His Spirit to bring it forth (Matt. 22:37; Rev. 22:17).

When Jesus spoke to His disciples of what we now know so well as the Lord's Prayer, He gave the very heartbeat behind our longing for His coming. We are to pray to our Father that His kingdom would come, His will would be done on earth as it is in heaven (Matt. 6:9–10). Herein lies the tension of our great yearning. We are those caught between two ages, and we await the convergence of the two. Our home and our inheritance are not found in the world as we know it. We are betrothed to a Bridegroom who is the King. Until the time when Jesus returns and establishes His kingdom on the earth, our prayer daily, our constant posture of heart, is to live as citizens of the coming kingdom, crying out for a changing-over of the government of this earth.

The King will surely come. At His coming, this One we love with all of our hearts will judge the nations, bind the Evil One, deliver His people, restore the whole earth, and be worshiped as

King over the nations (Ps. 2; 86:9; 110; Jer. 3:17; Dan. 7:14). Until then, we mourn and long for Him, embracing hunger for Him at the heart level. The same instinctive response that the apostles of the Lamb knew, that of radical yearning and radical living, is where the Lord will bring any willing heart in this hour.

The King's Appearing

Once again, as I use my imagination, I see a glimpse of our Lord's appearing. Come with me through this potential narrative of His return.

A deep darkness covers the earth as the light of the sun is dimmed and the moon does not give its light. Believers across the earth who have survived all manner of persecution and tribulation are imprisoned, condemned to die, hated by all men. They are despised and rejected.

Israel is once again backed up against an impossible wall as the evil man of sin and his armies close in and surround her with a vengeance, demonically energized by Satan's infuriated zeal to stop the second coming by keeping this nation from receiving their true King (Rev. 12:7–15). The earth has undergone severe distress and great perplexity with the sea and the waves roaring and the powers of the heavens being shaken (Hag. 2:6; Heb. 12:26–27). Men's hearts are failing them for fear and the expectation of what is coming by the hand of God (Luke 21:25–26).

The peoples of the earth have been traumatized and desensitized by every manner of false signs and lying wonders, false christs and so-called deliverers (Matt. 24:4–5). The nations have come under a deception of so-called peace and safety, which is marked by an evil convergence of the religions of the world—namely a syncretism of Christianity, Islam, and Judaism (1 Thess. 5:3). A strong delusion has seized the hearts of those who did not receive the love of the truth, and the hearts of many far and wide have grown cold (Matt. 24:12; 2 Thess. 2:11).

Yet all over the earth, just as Jesus foretold, witnesses within the Body of Christ, bondservants of Jesus, stand in victory amid the great onslaught of darkness. Not loving their lives, even at the threat of losing them, they are triumphant in love, alive in the Holy Spirit and His power, having dreams and visions, with demonstrations of power giving witness to the coming King (Joel 2:28–29). These victorious ones all across the earth and from every tribe and nation are now looking up, lifting their heads heavenward with holy expectation and fervent love because all has transpired just as He foretold, leaving only the greatest marvel and most awesome sight ever to be witnessed by the eyes of men—the return of the great King.

And *then*, the great and holy *then* of God, a *"suddenly"* determined from before the worlds were formed—*then* comes the sign in heaven of the Son of Man. At the splitting wide of the sky, behold, the great King appears on the clouds of heaven with power and great glory (Matt. 24:30; Luke 21:27; Rev. 1:7). He comes with all the shattering beauty of transcendent majesty, piercing the veil of this trembling age and opening the broad door into the marvelous age to come. He who rides on the heaven of heavens, which were of old, comes as lightning from the east that flashes to the west (Ps. 68:33; Matt. 24:27).

And oh, how deeply personal is this King's appearing to each individual! It is not simply a generalized visitation that He demonstrates, but an appearance within the personal view of each soul on the earth. And riding upon the high clouds from east to west, over each region of every people of the entire inhabited world, He shows forth His majesty until, progressively, every eye beholds Him and each in turn beholds His mighty appearing (Rev. 1:7).

Looking up with natural eyes to behold the marvelous and terrifying sight of a real Man, who is God in the flesh, robed in great power, and descending with flaming fire and the Father's glory, every person witnesses with terrifying wonder His magnificent appearing (Matt. 16:27; Mark 13:26). He descends with a shout, the voice of an archangel, and with the trumpet of God, raising the dead upon His arrival (1 Thess. 4:14–16). And at this thunderous return, as He comes to be glorified in His saints and admired among all those who believe, a great silence seizes and encompasses the earth as all men marvel and all are still before Him, for surely *He is God* (Ps. 46:10).

Expectant and faith-filled hearts of believers in Jesus everywhere—the shattered of the earth, whose very lives have been loathed, detested, and abhorred; the poor and lowly ones who have been ground into the dust under the heavy hand of persecution—fix their eyes upon Him, for it is for them that *He comes*. These He will deliver and exalt. For just as He promised, it will be the righteous lives of the meek and the lowly who will inherit the earth and rule with Him (Ps. 37:11, 39; Isa. 11:4; Dan. 7:18, 27; Matt. 5:5; 13:43; 1 Cor. 6:2). These righteous and meek ones of the earth now lift their faces upward to see with naked eye that which they have only ever believed with the eyes of faith (1 Cor. 13:12). And like a Bridegroom coming out of His chamber and rejoicing as a strong man to run his race, behold, our Redeemer (Ps. 19:5)! Behold the King of kings and Lord of lords; He comes with power and great glory! And His reward is with Him (Isa. 62:11; Rev. 22:12). He is mighty to save! Oh, glorious day for the righteous! For when the trumpet sounds, the dead shall be raised incorruptible, and we shall all be changed (1 Cor. 15:32)!

All of the saints who formerly died and now accompany the King in His descent from out of the ivory palaces are clothed *first* with bodies immortal as every grave opens to give up the dead (Ps. 45:8; 1 Thess. 4:16). As the great procession in the sky unfolds, those saints who are alive on the earth at His return see King Jesus coming in the clouds with power and great glory. Suddenly, they are wondrously caught up in the air, joining the Mighty One and all who are with Him in the air (1 Cor. 15:51–52). What a magnificent wonder as they rise! For in the twinkling of an eye, watch as each saint is changed and caught up to meet his Lord. Their earthly tent clothed eternal, from corruptible to incorruptible. As every persecutor and every adversary watches in horrific amazement, the weak ones are made strong, and the sons of God are revealed (Rom. 8:19). And behold! The stunning reunion in the sky, as all who are alive at His return are caught up and reunited with those saints formerly asleep, convening in the clouds as they join the Lord in the air, always and forever to be with Him (Col. 3:4; 1 Thess. 2:19–20; 4:13–18; 1 John 3:2–3)! With glorious procession, the angels of God are sent by Jesus to gather together His elect from the four winds, from one end of the sky to the other, from one end of heaven to the other (Matt. 24:30–31).

Descending from heaven and resting His foot upon the earth, He rides forth victoriously through the land, followed by angels and resurrected saints, with eyes fixed like flint once more toward Jerusalem. His heart is set to deliver Israel, His brethren in the flesh, in the old City. He has gone this way before (Isa. 50:7). This time He faces not a cross but a throne (Isa. 19:1; Hos. 11:1). This time the crowd that once cried, "Crucify Him!" will proclaim of the same Man, "Blessed is He who comes in the name of the Lord to deliver us!" (Luke 13:35; 23:21; John 19:5).

He comes to vindicate and glorify His saints. He comes to save Israel (Isa. 62:11–12; Zech. 9:16; Rom. 11:25–32). He comes to defeat and destroy the powers of darkness (Gen. 3:15; Rev. 19–20). He comes to condemn the wicked (Dan. 12:2; Matt. 25:31; John 5:27–30; Rev. 20). He comes to reward the righteous (Dan. 12; 1 Cor. 3:12–15). He comes to take His place as King on His holy hill of Zion and establish His kingdom forever (1 Cor. 15:23–28; Rev. 20–22). He comes to declare the decree His Father has spoken, "Ask of Me, and I will give You the nations for Your inheritance, and the ends of the earth for Your possession. You shall break them with a rod of iron; You shall dash them to pieces like a potter's vessel" (Ps. 2:6–9). *The King has returned!* Let all the earth tremble before Him.

Our Blessed Hope

The most glorious story ever to be revealed, spoken, or heard has yet to reach its culmination. And it is *our* story. The day that the Lord snatched us from the fire and made us His own, marking and sealing us by His Spirit, we became part of a drama so grand, so awesome, and so holy. The story of redemptive history that began at creation and thundered at the incarnation and the cross *will* culminate when the One who now sits at the right hand of God rends the heavens and comes down. How personal to us is that blessed day! The One we love, the One we have yearned for, the One we have set all our affections upon and laid all our treasure in *is alive*. And He is not staying where He is, but will soon come again to us and receive us to Himself (1 Pet. 1:3–9). This time He is not coming for a moment, but He is coming to stay. The God-man is returning in a human, glorified body to rule and reign. He will take His place as King over all the earth and His kingdom will know no end (Isa. 9:7; Dan. 7:14). This is our blessed hope.

Our hope is not anchored in the highest that today might hold or the best unfolding that we could imagine for our lives. Amid the rise and fall of circumstances and the roller coaster of our days, our hope is anchored in this future day—immovable and certain. When our hope rests fully upon the grace that is to come to us when Christ is revealed in His glory, then all of life works as it should. Our yearnings are set upon the One who will one day meet them in utter fullness. Our affections are riveted upon the One most worthy of all affection—the only One able to receive and rightly handle the passions of the human heart. Truly we were made for this ordering of our vision upon eternity and this setting of our affections upon Christ.

We live today in a fallen age and in a world lying under the sway of the ruler of darkness (1 John 5:19). The day upon which we have set our hope fully will be a day beyond comprehension. We were forgiven and redeemed for a purpose. We were saved for a reason. Jesus will return and bring forth that glorious intention as He brings forth in us the picture of His glory—those in His likeness, filled with love and bright righteousness.

Paul called the second coming of Jesus the Church's blessed

hope and exhorted us to comfort one another with this (1 Thess. 4:13–18; Titus 2:13). On that day, we will be given our resurrected bodies, and finally, our clouded and doubting minds will be filled with light (1 Cor. 15:51). We will at last entirely cast off the body of sin, and our emotions will be stripped of their stains. Finally, we will be holy in pure and perfect love for God and one another. With His return will come the ending of temptations, and at long last the warring will be done. Finally, we will live just as we were formed and fashioned to live.

Within this great ending of the story, the culmination that will instigate a whole new age and a whole new beginning, the long-awaited wedding day will finally come. The Lord Jesus will return for His Bride, and the days of betrothal, the days of waiting and yearning, the days of expecting and continually fighting to keep our hearts in the fires of devotion and out of the cold of dullness will come to a close. The Lord our Bridegroom will come to receive us to Himself just as He promised, and what began as a legal contract with holy vows and subsequent long delays will ultimately and at long last be consummated.

On that day, we, the Church and the Bride of the Lamb, will stand together on the sea of glass with all unity, all beauty, and all glory. We will declare how exceedingly perfect the Lord's leadership was over our lives and all of human history. Our eyes will behold with brilliant clarity the masterpiece of God's tapestry of time, and we will behold His glorious and excellent leadership in working all things together for the supreme good. We will see how every single aspect of our lives, every individual day, and every separate circumstance were arranged to bring forth a prepared Bride for the Son of God. We will marvel at the precision in Christ's leadership as He orchestrated all of history and every generation to bring to fullness the desire of His heart from the beginning of time.

As we behold this majestic leadership of the Son of God, the groaning of our earthly lives will be transformed into an awesome thunderous voice of worship. As all of time culminates in this triumphant marriage supper of the Lamb, the greatest event of all history, we will declare with a voice like the sound of many waters and of mighty thundering, "Alleluia! For the Lord God Omnipotent reigns! Let us be glad and rejoice and give Him glory, for the marriage of the Lamb has come and His wife has made herself ready" (Rev. 19:6–7).

Conclusion

Standing between the two comings of Christ, we have set our hope fully on the return of Jesus and the grace that is to be brought to us on that day (1 Pet. 1:13–16). During this time frame, we continually hold precious the Person who came and walked among us and gave His life for us, living in eager expectation of His return. "Christ was offered once to bear the sins of many. To those who eagerly wait for Him He will appear a second time, apart from sin, for salvation" (Heb. 9:28).

At the end of his life, Paul promised that this yearning and longing for Jesus' return would not be in vain but would be recognized, honored, and rewarded. He promised all who would posture their hearts and lives with a groan, all who would embrace the holy ache, a crown of righteousness laid up for them—a specific crown reserved for all who longed for and loved the Lord's appearing (2 Tim. 4:8). This is our calling and our holy longing, to possess and be possessed by God. We are His friends. We are His Bride. He is our God, and He is our Bridegroom. We have seen Him. We have beheld His glory. He has wounded and won our hearts with His love, His tenderness, His kindness, and His jealousy. He has anchored our hope in Himself, His coming, and His kingdom. With Paul, our hearts and lives incessantly exclaim, "Maranatha! O Lord, come!" and with John, we continually cry, "Amen. Even so, come, Lord Jesus!" (1 Cor. 16:22; Rev. 22:20). Until that Day, we *long, mourn,* and *fast* for Him.

Works Cited

Bickle, Mike, and Dana Candler. *The Rewards of Fasting: Experiencing the Power and Affections of God.* Kansas City: Forerunner Books, 2005.

Cross, St. John of the. *The Collected Works of St. John of the Cross.* Washington, D.C.: ICS Publications, 1991.

Liguori, St. Alphonsus. *The Practice of the Love of Jesus Christ.* United States of America: Liguori Publications, 1997.

Dubay, Thomas. *Deep Conversion, Deep Prayer.* San Francisco: Ignatius Press, 2006.

Dubay, Thomas. *The Evidential Power of Beauty: Science and Theology Meet.* San Francisco: Ignatius Press, 1999.

Dubay, Thomas. "Thirst for Our God." Online audio teaching. <http://www.ewtn.com/vondemand/audio/file_index.asp?SeriesId=840549426&pgnu>.

Grudem, Wayne. *Systematic Theology: An Introduction to Biblical Theology.* Grand Rapids: Zondervan, 1994.

Nouwen, Henri. *Bread for the Journey.* San Francisco: Harper, 1997.

Piper, John. *A Hunger for God: Desiring God through Fasting and Prayer.* Wheaton: Crossway Books, 1997.

Tozer, A. W. *The Pursuit of God.* Camp Hill: Christian Publications, Inc., 1948.

Venable, Stephen, *The Life of Christ in the Gospels.* International House of Prayer University. Session 04, 2008.

International House of Prayer
Missions Base

....

24/7 Live Worship and Prayer
IHOP.org

....

Since September 19, 1999, we have continued in night and day prayer with worship as the foundation of our ministry to win the lost, heal the sick, and make disciples as we labor alongside the larger Body of Christ to see the Great Commission fulfilled and to function as forerunners who prepare the way for the return of Jesus. By the grace of God, we are committed to combining 24/7 prayers for justice with 24/7 works for justice until the Lord returns. We do this best as our lives are rooted in prayer that focuses on intimacy with God and intercession for breakthrough of the fullness of God's power and purpose for this generation.

For more information on our internships, conferences, university, live prayer room webcast, and more, please visit our website at IHOP.org.

International House of Prayer Missions Base
3535 E. Red Bridge Road, Kansas City, MO 64137
816.763.0200 • info@ihop.org • IHOP.org

IHOPU

International House of Prayer University

....

Ministry, Music, Media, and eSchool
IHOP.org/university

....

The International House of Prayer University (IHOPU) is a full-time Bible school which exists to equip this generation in the knowledge of God and the power of the Spirit for the bold proclamation of the Lord Jesus and His return.

Students embrace rigorous theological training and Sermon on the Mount lifestyles in the context of a thriving missions base fueled by night and day prayer (IHOP–KC). As a result, theological education obtained in the classroom is intrinsically connected to intimacy with Jesus and hands-on experience.

IHOPU is distinct from many other institutions of higher learning in the United States in that we seek a holistic approach to education with an emphasis on the forerunner ministry, and a NightWatch training element. IHOPU is led by intercessory missionaries in an environment of night and day prayer and a thriving missions base.

International House of Prayer University
3535 E. Red Bridge Road, Kansas City, MO 64137
816.763.0243 • ihopu@ihop.org • IHOP.org/university